DISCOVERING FRENCH BLEU

**Communicative Expressions
and Thematic Vocabulary**

Jean-Paul Valette
Rebecca Valette

D.C. Heath and Company,
a Division of Houghton Mifflin Company

HEATH

Contents

To the Student

Your Activity Book is divided into five units. Each unit has four sections:

Listening Activities

The Listening Activities (called Cassette Worksheets) have the pictures you will need to complete the recorded activities. The 20 lessons correspond to the 20 lessons in the student text. When you work with the Cassette Program, you will need your textbook as well as your Activity Book with you, so that you can follow along for the vocabulary sections and the À **votre tour** sections.

Writing Activities

The Writing Activities will give you the chance to develop your writing skills and put into practice what you have learned in class. The 20 lessons correspond to the 20 lessons in the student text. Starting in Unit 4, the exercises are coded to correspond to a particular part of the lesson. For example, **A** at the beginning of an exercise or group of exercises means that the material is related to the structures or vocabulary presented in Section A of that lesson. The last activity is called **Communication** and encourages you to express yourself in various additional communicative situations.

Reading and Culture Activities

The Reading and Culture Activities contain realia (illustrations and objects from real life) from French-speaking countries and various kinds of cultural activities. There is one set of activities for each unit in the student text.

Communicative Expressions and Thematic Vocabulary

The **Pour Communiquer** section summarizes all of the vocabulary introduced in the lessons of each unit. The words and expressions are grouped into categories that will make it easier for you to review the material.

UNITÉ 1
Bonjour!

LISTENING ACTIVITIES
Leçons 1–4

WRITING ACTIVITIES
Leçons 1–4

READING AND CULTURE ACTIVITIES
Unité 1

Communicative Expressions and Thematic Vocabulary

Nom ____

Classe _________________________________ Date _____________

CASSETTE WORKSHEET Leçon 1 La rentrée

Section 1 | La rentrée *(Back to school)*

A. *Compréhension orale.* Listening comprehension.

This is the first day of school. Students are greeting their friends and meeting new classmates.

PHILIPPE: Bonjour! Je m'appelle Philippe.
STÉPHANIE: Et moi, je m'appelle Stéphanie.
MARC: Je m'appelle Marc. Et toi?
ISABELLE: Moi, je m'appelle Isabelle.
JEAN-PAUL: Comment t'appelles-tu?
NATHALIE: Je m'appelle Nathalie.
JEAN-PAUL: Bonjour.
NATHALIE: Bonjour.

B. *Écoutez et répétez.* Listen and repeat.

Section 2 | Qui est-ce? *(Who is it?)*

C. *Compréhension orale.* Listening comprehension.

▶ (a.) François
b. Frank

1. a. Nathalie
b. Nicole

2. a. Sylvie
b. Cécile

3. a. Jean-Claude
b. Jean-Paul

4. a. Lucie
b. Juliette

UNITÉ 1

CASSETTE WORKSHEET   Leçon 1   (cont.)

D. *Compréhension orale.* Listening comprehension.

a. ____ Monsieur Fazère   **f.** ____ Charles Dumont

b. ____ Olivier LeGrand   **g.** ____ Monsieur Martin

c. _1_ Florence Clément   **h.** ____ Monsieur Ronchon

d. ____ Madame Bertin   **i.** ____ Jeanne Dupont

e. ____ Mademoiselle Lacour

E. *Compréhension orale.* Listening comprehension.

1. a. ____ Michèle   b. ____ Hélène

2. a. ____ Fatou   b. ____ Nicolas

3. a. ____ Paul   b. ____ Loriza

Section 3   **L'alphabet et les signes orthographiques**
(The alphabet and spelling marks)

F. *Écoutez et répétez.* Listen and repeat.

> A B C D E F G H I J K L M
> N O P Q R S T U V W X Y Z

G. *Écoutez et répétez.* Listen and repeat.

/ accent aigu   **Cécile**   **··** tréma   **Noël**

**** accent grave   **Michèle**   **ç** cédille   **François**

^ accent circonflexe   **Jérôme**

Nom ____

CASSETTE WORKSHEET   Leçon 1   (cont.)

H. *Écoutez et écrivez.* Listen and write.

1. ___ ___ ___ ___

2. ___ ___ ___ ___ ___

3. ___ ___ ___ ___ ___

4. ___ ___ ___ ___ ___

5. ___ ___ ___ ___ ___ ___ ___

Section 4   **Les nombres de 0 à 10** *(Numbers from 0 to 10)*

I. *Écoutez et répétez.* Listen and repeat.

0 (zéro)	1 (un)	2 (deux)	3 (trois)	4 (quatre)	5 (cinq)
6 (six)	7 (sept)	8 (huit)	9 (neuf)	10 (dix)	

J. *Écoutez et écrivez.* Listen and write.

Éric: ___ ___ ___ - ___ ___ ___

Marie: ___ ___ ___ - ___ ___ ___

Jean-Jacques: ___ ___ ___ - ___ ___ ___

Nom ____

Classe _________________________________ Date _____________

CASSETTE WORKSHEET Leçon 2 Tu es français?

Section 1 **Tu es français?** *(You're French?)*

A. *Compréhension orale*

> *It is the opening day of school and several of the students meet in the cafeteria at lunchtime. Marc discovers that not everyone is French.*
>
> MARC: Tu es français?
> JEAN-PAUL: Oui, je suis français.
> MARC: Et toi, Patrick, tu es français aussi?
> PATRICK: Non! Je suis américain. Je suis de Boston.
> MARC: Et toi, Stéphanie, tu es française ou américaine?
> STÉPHANIE: Je suis française.
> MARC: Tu es de Paris?
> STÉPHANIE: Non, je suis de Fort-de-France.
> MARC: Tu as de la chance!

B. *Écoutez et répétez.* Listen and repeat.

Section 2 **Quelle nationalité?** *(What nationality?)*

C. *Compréhension orale*

		▶	1	2	3	4	5	6	7	8
A	**français**	✓								
B	**française**									

UNITÉ 1

CASSETTE WORKSHEET Leçon 2 (cont.)

D. *Compréhension orale*

	A	B	C	D	E	F
	anglais	anglaise	américain	américaine	canadien	canadienne
▶					✓	
1						
2						
3						
4						
5						
6						
7						

E. *Compréhension orale*

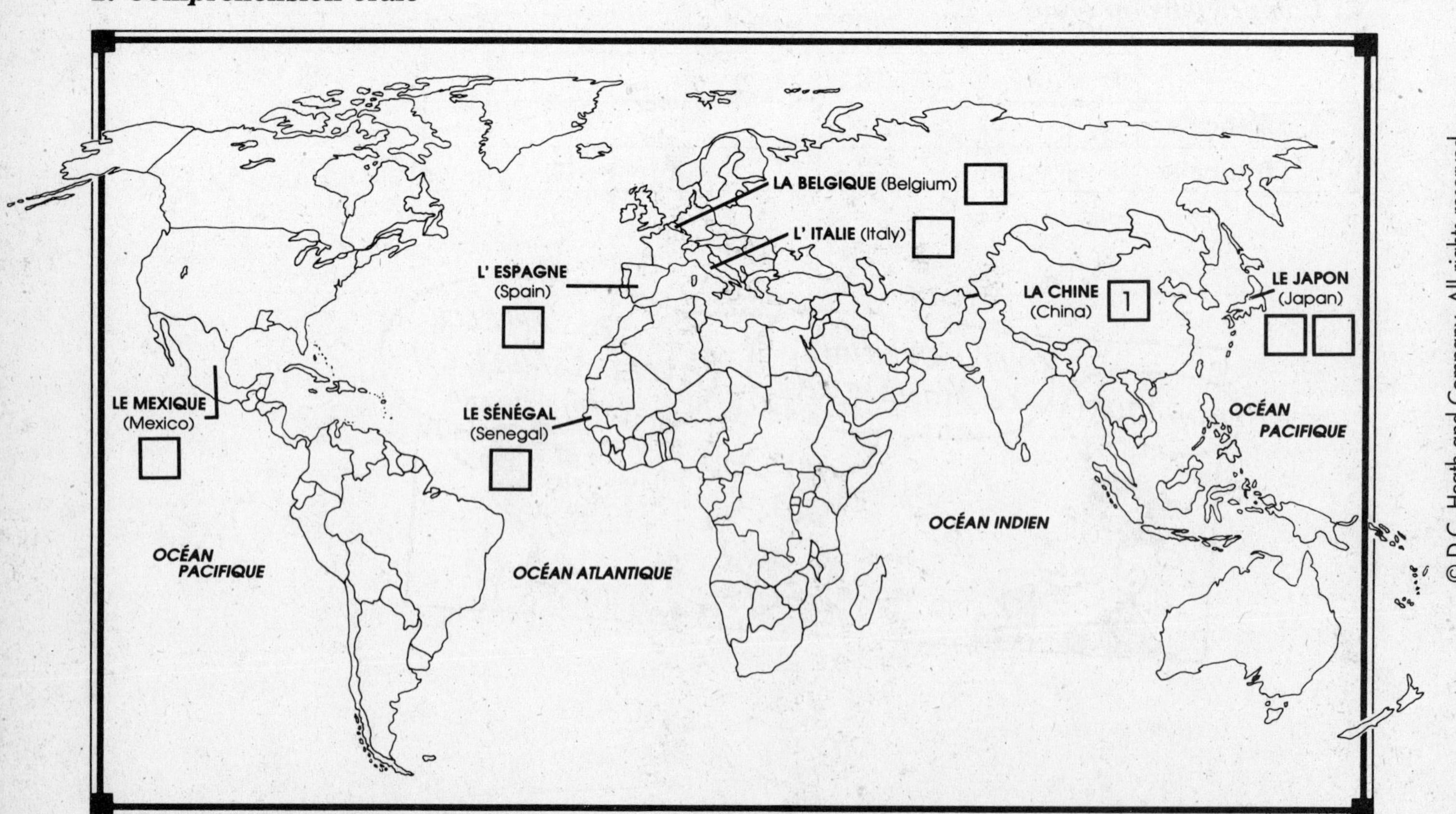

DISCOVERING FRENCH – *BLEU*

UNITÉ 1

CASSETTE WORKSHEET   Leçon 2   (cont.)

Section 3 | **Les nombres de 10 à 20**

F. *Écoutez et répétez.* Listen and repeat.

> **10** (dix) **11** (onze) **12** (douze) **13** (treize) **14** (quatorze) **15** (quinze)
>
> **16** (seize) **17** (dix-sept) **18** (dix-huit) **19** (dix-neuf) **20** (vingt)

G. *Écoutez et écrivez.* Listen and write.

▶ 
Philippe

Paul

François

Marc

Jérôme

Jean-Michel

Frédéric

Patrick

Robert

Thomas

UNITÉ 1

CASSETTE WORKSHEET   Leçon 2 (cont.)

| Section 4 | **Prononciation** |

H. *Les lettres muettes* (Silent letters)
Écoutez: **Paris**
In French, the last letter of a word is often not pronounced.

- Final "**e**" is always silent.

  Répétez: **Sophie   Philippe   Stéphanie   anglaise   française
  onze   douze   treize   quatorze   quinze   seize**

- Final "**s**" is almost always silent.

  Répétez: **Paris   Nicolas   Jacques   anglais   français   trois**

- The letter "**h**" is always silent.

  Répétez: **Hélène   Henri   Thomas   Nathalie   Catherine**

Nom _______________________________

Classe _______________________________ Date _______________

CASSETTE WORKSHEET Leçon 3 Salut! Ça va?

| Section 1 | **Salut! Ça va?** |

A. *Compréhension orale*

On the way to school, François meets his friends.

FRANÇOIS: Salut, Isabelle!
ISABELLE: Salut! Ça va?
FRANÇOIS: Ça va! Merci!

FRANÇOIS: Salut, Nathalie! Ça va?
NATHALIE: Ça va bien! Et toi?
FRANÇOIS: Moi aussi.

ISABELLE: Ça va, Philippe?
PHILIPPE: Ah non! Zut! Ça va mal!

François also meets his teachers.

FRANÇOIS: Bonjour, monsieur.
M. MASSON: Bonjour, François.

FRANÇOIS: Bonjour, madame.
MME CHOLLET: Bonjour, François.

FRANÇOIS: Bonjour, mademoiselle.
MLLE LACOUR: Bonjour, François.

After class, François says good-bye to his teacher and his friends.

FRANÇOIS: Au revoir, mademoiselle.
MLLE LACOUR: Au revoir, François.

NATHALIE: Au revoir, François.
FRANÇOIS: Au revoir, Nathalie.

B. *Écoutez et répétez.* Listen and repeat.

| Section 2 | **Ça va?** |

C. *Compréhension orale*

Ça va bien!

a. ____

Ça va très bien!

b. ____

Ça va comme ci, comme ça.

c. ____

Ça va mal.

d. ____

Ça va très mal.

e. ____

UNITÉ 1

CASSETTE WORKSHEET   Leçon 3   (cont.)

D. *Questions et réponses*

▶ —Ça va?

—Ça va comme ci, comme ça.

CASSETTE WORKSHEET   Leçon 3   (cont.)

Section 3   Les nombres de 20 à 60

E. *Écoutez et répétez.* Listen and repeat.

20	21	22	23	24	25	26
27	28	29	30	31	32	33 . . .
40	41 . . .		44	45	46 . . .	
50	51 . . .		57	58	59	60

F. *Écoutez et écrivez.* Listen and write.

Louis Bertrand ____ ____ . ____ ____ . ____ ____ . ____ ____ . ____ ____

Marie-Claire Dulac ____ ____ . ____ ____ . ____ ____ . ____ ____ . ____ ____

Charles Leclerc ____ ____ . ____ ____ . ____ ____ . ____ ____ . ____ ____

Stéphanie Ladoux ____ ____ . ____ ____ . ____ ____ . ____ ____ . ____ ____

UNITÉ 1

CASSETTE WORKSHEET   Leçon 3   (cont.)

Section 4   **Prononciation**

G. *Les consonnes finales* (Final consonants)

Écoutez: **un   deux   trois**

In French, the last consonant of a word is often not pronounced.

- Remember: Final "**s**" is usually silent.

  Répétez: **trois   français   anglais**

- Most other final consonants are usually silent.

  Répétez: **Richard   Albert   Robert   salut
                américain   canadien   bien   deux**

EXCEPTION: The following final consonants are usually pronounced:
"**c**," "**f**," "**l**," and sometimes "**r**."

  Répétez: **Éric   Daniel   Lebeuf   Pascal   Victor**

However, the ending **-er** is usually pronounced /e/.

  Répétez: **Roger   Olivier**

CASSETTE WORKSHEET Leçon 4   Le français pratique: L'heure

Section 1   **Dialogue A: Un rendez-vous**

A. *Compréhension orale*

Jean-Paul and Stéphanie are sitting in a café. Stéphanie seems to be in a hurry to leave.

STÉPHANIE: Quelle heure est-il?
JEAN-PAUL: Il est trois heures.
STÉPHANIE: Trois heures?
JEAN-PAUL: Oui, trois heures.
STÉPHANIE: Oh là là. J'ai un rendez-vous avec David dans vingt minutes.
Au revoir, Jean-Paul.
JEAN-PAUL: Au revoir, Stéphanie. À bientôt!

B. *Écoutez et répétez.*

Section 2   **Quelle heure est-il?** (Part 1)

C. *Compréhension orale*

1.   **2.**   **3.**   **4.**   **5.**

D. *Questions et réponses*

1.   **2.**   **3.**   **4.**

5.   **6.**   **7.**

UNITÉ 1

CASSETTE WORKSHEET   Leçon 4   (cont.)

Section 3 | **Dialogue B: À quelle heure est le film?**

E. *Compréhension orale*

> *Stéphanie and David have decided to go to a movie.*
>
> STÉPHANIE: Quelle heure est-il?
>   DAVID: Il est trois heures et demie.
> STÉPHANIE: Et à quelle heure est le film?
>   DAVID: À quatre heures et quart.
> STÉPHANIE: Ça va. Nous avons le temps.

F. *Écoutez et répétez.*

Section 4 | **Quelle heure est-il?** (Part 2)

G. *Compréhension orale*

1. 2.

3. 4.

H. *Questions et réponses*

 1.

 2.

 4.

 5.

 6.

UNITÉ 1

CASSETTE WORKSHEET Leçon 4 (cont.)

Section 5 | À quelle heure?

I. *Compréhension orale*

▶ le film _____4 h 15_____

1. la classe de français _________

2. le dîner _________

3. le film _________

4. le train de Toulouse _________

Section 6 | L'heure officielle

J. *Compréhension orale*

▶ | 17 h 00 |

– 12
| 5:00 P.M. |

1. | | **2.** | | **3.** | |

– 12   – 12   – 12
| | | | | |

UNITÉ 1

CASSETTE WORKSHEET Leçon 4 (cont.)

À votre tour!

Section 1. Nathalie et Marc

Allez à la page 30. *Turn to page 30 in your Student Text.*

Section 2. Et toi?

Allez à la page 30.

Section 3. Conversation dirigée

Allez à la page 30.

Section 4. Minidialogues

Allez à la page 31.

Nom ____

Classe _________________________________ Date _____________

WRITING ACTIVITIES Leçon 1   La rentrée

1. Au Club International

You have met the following young people at the Club International.
Six of them have names of French origin. Circle these names. Then
write them in the box below, separating the boys and the girls.
(Note: Don't forget the accent marks!)

Carlos Suárez	Mustapha Ibrahim
Birgit Eriksen	Jérôme Dupuis
Hélène Rémy	Janet Woodford
Jean-François Petit	Raúl González
Michiko Sato	Marie-Noëlle Laîné
Frédéric Lemaître	Svetlana Poliakoff
Heinz Mueller	Stéphanie Mercier

FLASH culturel

French is spoken not only in France. Today about thirty countries
use French as their official language (or one of their official
languages). Which continent has the largest number of French-
speaking countries?

☐ Europe   ☐ Africa   ☐ Asia   ☐ South America

➜ **page 20**

WRITING ACTIVITIES Leçon 1 (cont.)

2. Allô!

First write down your phone number and the numbers of two friends or relatives.
Then write out the numbers as you would say them in French.

1. Moi

☐ ☐ ☐–☐ ☐ ☐ ☐

______/______/______/ – /______/______/______/

2. Nom *(name)*: ______________________________

☐ ☐ ☐–☐ ☐ ☐ ☐

______/______/______/ – /______/______/______/

3. Nom *(name)*: ______________________________

☐ ☐ ☐–☐ ☐ ☐ ☐

______/______/______/ – /______/______/______/

3. Communication: En français!

On the bus you meet a new French student. Write out what you
would say — in French!

1. *Say hello.*

____

2. *Give your name.*

____

3. *Ask the French student his/her name.*

____

FLASH culturel

French is the official language in 25 African countries. The largest
of these countries is Zaïre in central Africa. Other countries where
French is spoken by many of the citizens are: Algeria, Tunisia, and
Morocco in North Africa; Senegal and the Ivory Coast in West
Africa; and the island of Madagascar off the coast of East Africa.

WRITING ACTIVITIES Leçon 2 Tu es français?

1. Présentations *(Introductions)*

The following people are introducing themselves, giving their names and their nationalities.
Complete what each one says.

Je m'appelle Cédric.

Je suis _______________.

Je m'appelle Liz.

Je suis _______________.

Je m'appelle Tina.

Je suis _______________.

Je m'appelle Pierre.

Je suis _______________.

Je m'appelle Bob.

Je suis _______________.

Je m'appelle Véronique.

Je suis _______________.

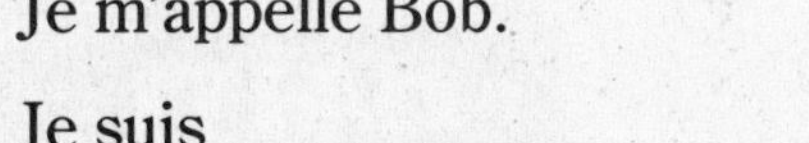

FLASH culturel

Martinique and Guadeloupe are two French-speaking islands in the
Caribbean. In which other Caribbean country is French spoken?

☐ Cuba   ☐ Puerto Rico   ☐ Haiti   ☐ The Dominican Republic

➡ **page 22**

WRITING ACTIVITIES Leçon 2 (cont.)

2. Maths

Write out the answers to the following arithmetic problems.

▶ 4 + 7 = _onze_

1. 9 + 3 = _______________
2. 8 + 6 = _______________
3. 10 + 7 = _______________

4. 17 + 2 = _______________
5. 5 x 3 = _______________
6. 2 x 10 = _______________

3. Communication: En français!

You are at a party and have just met two French-speaking students:
Philippe and Marie-Laure.

1. *Say hello to them.*

____

2. *Give your name.*

____

3. *Say that you are American.*

____

4. *Ask Philippe if he is French.*

____

5. *Ask Marie-Laure if she is Canadian.*

____

FLASH culturel

· B O S T O N ·
HAÏTI
COURRIER

Haiti is a former French colony. Toward the end of the eighteenth
century, the black slaves who worked in the sugar cane plantations
revolted against their French masters. In 1804, Haiti became an
independent country. It is the first republic established by people of
African origin.

Today French, which is the official language of Haiti, is spoken by
many Haitians, along with Creole. Many people of Haitian origin
live in the United States, especially in Florida, New York, and
Boston. If you meet young Haitians, you might want to speak
French with them.

UNITÉ 1

WRITING ACTIVITIES Leçon 3 Salut! Ça va?

1. Loto *(Bingo)*

You are playing Loto in Quebec. The numbers below have all been called. If you have these numbers on your card, circle them.

seize	trente et un	vingt-deux	cinquante	quarante-neuf	quinze
quarante	trente-quatre	vingt-neuf	soixante	quarante-huit	douze
cinquante-deux	onze	dix-sept	vingt et un	vingt	trente-cinq
trente-sept	cinquante-six	sept	cinquante-quatre		
cinquante-neuf	trois				

5	14	26	37	49
7	15	29	40	52
9	18	X	41	54
11	21	33	46	59
12	22	35	48	60

How many numbers did you circle? _______________

How many rows of five did you score? _______________

FLASH culturel

France is not the only European country where French is spoken. In which of the following countries do one fifth of the people speak French?

☐ Germany ☐ Italy ☐ Spain ☐ Switzerland

→ page 24

UNITÉ 1

WRITING ACTIVITIES Leçon 3 (cont.)

2. Bonjour!

The following people meet in the street. How do you think they will greet each other?
Fill in the bubbles with the appropriate expressions.

Caroline Jérôme Mme Mercier Éric Mlle Bellamy M. Renaud

3. Ça va?

How do you think the following people would answer the question **Ça va?**

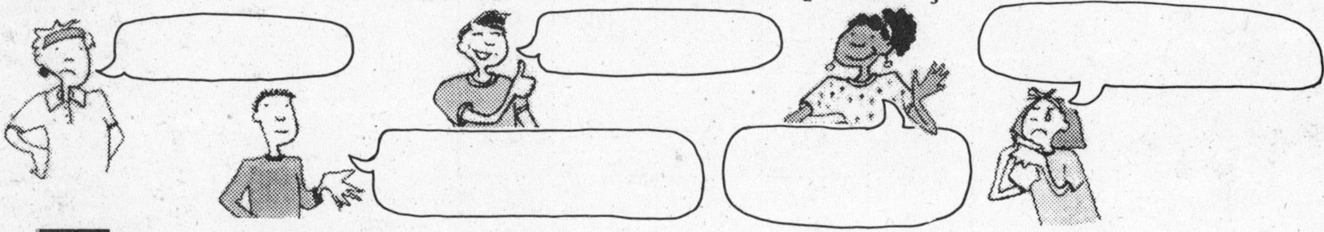

4. Communication: En français!

You have just enrolled in a French school as an exchange student.

1. On the way to school, you meet your friend Catherine.

    Say hello to her. ____

    Ask her how things are going. ____

2. Now you meet Mademoiselle Lebrun, your new music teacher.

    Say hello to her. ____

    Ask her how she is. ____

---

*F*LASH culturel

Although all of these countries border on France, only Switzerland
has a sizeable French-speaking population. The main French-
speaking city of Switzerland is Geneva **(Genève),** which is the
headquarters of the International Red Cross and the seat of several
other international organizations.

Nom ____

Classe _______________________________ Date _______________

WRITING ACTIVITIES Leçon 4 Le français pratique: L'heure

1. Oui ou non?

Watches do not always work well. Read the times below and compare them with the times indicated on the watches. If the two times match, check **oui.** If they do not match, check **non.**

		oui	non
▶	Il est une heure dix.	☐	☐
▶	Il est une heure vingt-cinq.	☐	☐
1.	Il est deux heures et demie.	☐	☐
2.	Il est trois heures et quart.	☐	☐
3.	Il est cinq heures moins vingt.	☐	☐
4.	Il est sept heures moins le quart.	☐	☐
5.	Il est huit heures cinq.	☐	☐
6.	Il est onze heures cinquante-cinq.	☐	☐

Flash culturel

In many French-speaking countries, official time is given using a 24-hour clock. For example, on this Canadian TV schedule, the movie *Driving Miss Daisy* begins at 22 h 40 (**vingt-deux heures quarante**). What would be the corresponding time on our 12-hour clock?

☐ 2:40 P.M.   ☐ 8:40 P.M.   ☐ 9:40 P.M.   ☐ 10:40 P.M.

Super Écran

VENDREDI 22 MARS

14h50	LAWRENCE D'ARABIE
18h20	ONCLE BUCK
20h05	LES SIMPSON
21h00	TREMORS
22h40	MISS DAISY ET SON CHAUFFEUR

➜ **page 26**

UNITÉ 1

WRITING ACTIVITIES Leçon 4 (cont.)

2. Quelle heure est-il?

Stéphanie's watch is not working. Tell her what time it is. Write out your responses.

1. _______________________________ .

2. _______________________________ .

3. _______________________________ .

`7:30`

4. _______________________________ .

`8:45`

5. _______________________________ .

`10:50`

6. _______________________________ .

3. Communication: En français!

A. Conversation avec Caroline   You are in a café with your friend Caroline. You plan to see a movie together. Complete the dialogue.

CAROLINE: Quelle heure est-il?

YOU: ______________________________________
(Look at your watch and tell her the time.)

CAROLINE: À quelle heure est le film?

YOU: ______________________________________
(Name a time about half an hour from now.)

B. Conversation avec Julien   You are in a hurry to keep an appointment with Mme Pascal, your math teacher. You meet your friend Julien. Complete the dialogue.

YOU: ______________________________________
(Ask Julien what time it is.)

JULIEN: Il est onze heures dix. Pourquoi *(why)*?

YOU: ________________________________ avec Madame Pascal.
(Say you have an appointment with Madame Pascal.)

JULIEN: À quelle heure?

YOU: ______________________________________
(Tell him at quarter past eleven, and say good-bye.)

FLASH culturel

With the 24-hour clock, times are expressed as follows:
- A.M. hours go from 0 h 01 (one minute after midnight) to 12 h 00 (noon).
- P.M. hours go from 12 h 01 to 24 h 00.

To calculate the P.M. equivalent of 24-hour clock times, simply subtract 12.

22 h 40 =
22:40 – 12 =
10:40 P.M.

READING AND CULTURE ACTIVITIES Unité 1

A. En voyage *(On a trip)*

1. Why would you go to Le Napoli?
- ☐ To shop for food.
- ☐ To have dinner.
- ☐ To see a movie.
- ☐ To plan a trip to Italy.

Le Napoli

**Restaurant - Pizzéria
Spécialités - Grillades**

7, Av. des Poilus - Place Cavet   ☎ 04 94 74 03 34
83110 Sanary-sur-mer

2. In which country is the Bonaparte located?
- ☐ In France.
- ☐ In Canada.
- ☐ In Switzerland.
- ☐ In Belgium.

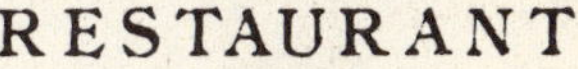

3. Why would you call the number shown in this ad?
- ☐ To buy a train ticket.
- ☐ To rent a video.
- ☐ To have your phone repaired.
- ☐ To reserve a room.

4. Why did someone buy this ticket?
- ☐ To visit a historical site.
- ☐ To see a historical movie.
- ☐ To listen to classical music.
- ☐ To tour a battleship.

UNITÉ 1

READING AND CULTURE ACTIVITIES   Unité 1 (cont.)

5. If you were in France, where would
you see this sign?
- ☐ In a train.
- ☐ In an elevator.
- ☐ On a highway.
- ☐ In a stadium.

6. If you were driving on this highway,
you would exit to the right . . .
- ☐ if you needed gas
- ☐ if you wanted to take pictures
- ☐ if you were looking for a campground
- ☐ if you were meeting a flight

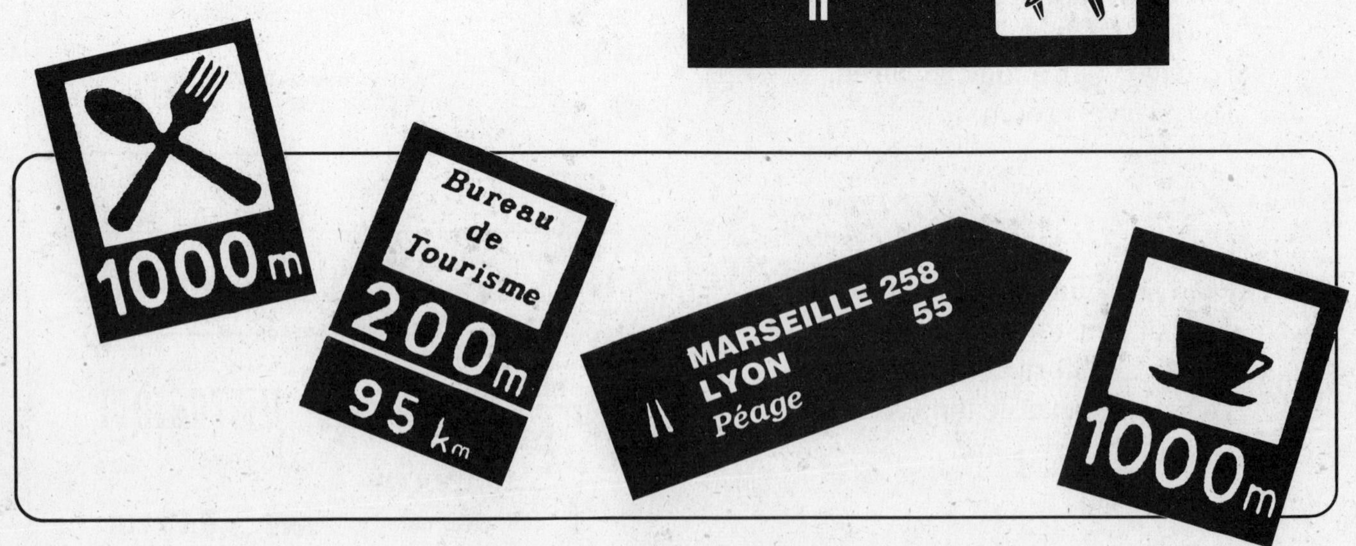

READING AND CULTURE ACTIVITIES Unité 1 (cont.)

B. Carte de visite

> **Marie-Françoise Bellanger**
>
> *photographe*
>
> *47, rue du Four*
> *Paris 6ᵉ*   *Tél. 01.42.21.30.15*

A friend of yours has given you the calling card of her cousin in
France. Fill in the blanks below with the information that you can
find out about this cousin by reading the card.

- Last name _______________________________
- First name _______________________________
- City of residence _______________________________
- Profession _______________________________

UNITÉ 1

READING AND CULTURE ACTIVITIES   Unité 1 (cont.)

C. Agenda

Look at the following page from Stéphanie's pocket calendar.

OCT.

SAMEDI **21**
(10) Octobre

42ᵉ Semaine

classe de piano 10 h 00

rendez-vous avec Jean-Paul 4 h 00

téléphoner à Christine 7 h 30

- What does Stéphanie have scheduled for Saturday morning at 10 A.M.?

  ____

- When is Stéphanie going to meet Jean-Paul?

  ____

- What is Stéphanie planning to do at 7:30?

  ____

COMMUNICATIVE EXPRESSIONS AND THEMATIC VOCABULARY
Unité 1 Bonjour!

▶ CULTURAL CONTEXT: **Meeting people**

COMMUNICATIVE EXPRESSIONS

Greeting people
Bonjour! **Au revoir!**
Salut!

Asking people how they are
(informally) **Ça va?** Ça va . . . | bien.
  Comment vas-tu? | mal
    | comme ci, comme ça
(formally) **Comment allez-vous?** | très bien
    | très mal

Asking a classmate's name
Comment t'appelles-tu?
  Je m'appelle . . .

Asking a friend which city he/she is from
Tu es de [Boston]?
  Je suis de [San Francisco].

Asking a friend about his/her nationality
Tu es . . . ? **français** **française**
  Je suis . . . **anglais** **anglaise**
    américain **américaine**
    canadien **canadienne**

Asking the time
Quelle heure est-il?
  Il est . . . **une heure** **midi**
    deux heures **minuit**
    trois heures et quart **neuf heures du matin**
    six heures et demie **cinq heures de l'après-midi**
    sept heures moins le quart **dix heures du soir**
    huit heures dix
    onze heures moins vingt

Asking at what time something begins
À quelle heure est . . . ?
  — À quelle heure est le concert?
  — Le concert est à huit heures.

Saying at what time you have an appointment or date
J'ai un rendez-vous à [quatre heures].

POUR COMMUNIQUER

COMMUNICATIVE EXPRESSIONS AND THEMATIC VOCABULARY

VOCABULARY

Numbers: 0–60

zéro	dix	vingt	trente
un	onze	vingt et un	
deux	douze	vingt-deux	quarante
trois	treize	vingt-trois	
quatre	quatorze	vingt-quatre	cinquante
cinq	quinze	vingt-cinq	
six	seize	vingt-six	soixante
sept	dix-sept	vingt-sept	
huit	dix-huit	vingt-huit	
neuf	dix-neuf	vingt-neuf	

Other expressions

oui	et	moi	Monsieur
non	ou	et toi?	Madame
merci	aussi		Mademoiselle
zut!			

UNITÉ 2
Les copains et la famille

LISTENING ACTIVITIES
Leçons 5–8

WRITING ACTIVITIES
Leçons 5–8

READING AND CULTURE ACTIVITIES
Unité 2

POUR COMMUNIQUER
Communicative Expressions and Thematic Vocabulary

Nom ____

Classe _________________________________ Date ___________

CASSETTE WORKSHEET Leçon 5 Copain ou copine?

Section 1 | Copain ou copine?

A. *Compréhension orale*

> *Today, Jean-Paul is visiting his friend Philippe. Philippe seems to be expecting someone.*
>
> PHILIPPE: Tiens! Voilà Dominique!
> JEAN-PAUL: Dominique? Qui est-ce? Un copain ou une copine?
> PHILIPPE: C'est une copine.
> PHILIPPE: Salut, Dominique! Ça va?
> DOMINIQUE: Oui, ça va! Et toi?
> JEAN-PAUL: C'est vrai! C'est une copine!

B. *Écoutez et répétez.*

Section 2 | Qui est-ce?

C. *Compréhension orale*

	A	B	C	D	E	F
	un ami	**une amie**	**un copain**	**une copine**	**un prof**	**une prof**
▶				✓		
1						
2						
3						
4						
5						

D. *Questions et réponses*

▶ — Tiens, voilà Isabelle!
— Qui est-ce?
— **C'est une copine.**

1. un copain? une copine?   **3.** un ami? une amie?   **5.** un prof? une prof?

2. un copain? une copine?   **4.** un ami? une amie?

CASSETTE WORKSHEET Leçon 5 (cont.)

UNITÉ 2

| Section 3 | **Les nombres de 60 à 79** |

E. *Écoutez et répétez.*

60	61	62	63	64	65	66	67	68	69
70	71	72	73	74	75	76	77	78	79

F. *Écoutez et écrivez.*

Jean-Michel Descroix ___ . ___ . ___ . ___ . ___

Christine Albert ___ . ___ . ___ . ___ . ___

Roger Boulanger ___ . ___ . ___ . ___ . ___

Mireille Chardin ___ . ___ . ___ . ___ . ___

| Section 4 | **Prononciation** |

G. *La liaison*

Écoutez: **un ami**
Répétez: **un ami   un Américain   un Anglais   un artiste**

In general, the "**n**" of **un** is silent. However, in the above words, the "**n**" of **un** is pronounced as if it were the first letter of the next word. The two words are linked together in LIAISON.

Liaison occurs between two words when the second one begins with a VOWEL SOUND, that is, with "**a**", "**e**", "**i**", "**o**", "**u**", and sometimes "**h**" and "**y**".

Contrastez et répétez:

    LIAISON: **un ami   un Américain   un Italien   un artiste**
    NO LIAISON: **un copain   un Français   un Canadien   un prof**

DISCOVERING FRENCH – *BLEU*

UNITÉ 2

CASSETTE WORKSHEET Leçon 6 Une coïncidence

Section 1 **Une coïncidence**

A. *Compréhension orale*

> *Isabelle is at a party with her new Canadian friend Mark. She wants him to meet some of the other guests.*
>
> ISABELLE: Tu connais la fille là-bas?
>
> MARC: Non. Qui est-ce?
>
> ISABELLE: C'est une copine. Elle s'appelle Juliette Savard.
>
> MARC: Elle est française?
>
> ISABELLE: Non, elle est canadienne. Elle est de Montréal.
>
> MARC: Moi aussi!
>
> ISABELLE: Quelle coïncidence!

B. *Écoutez et répétez.*

Section 2 **Qui est-ce?**

C. *Compréhension orale*

1. a. une amie   b. une copine
   c. Denise   d. Danielle
   e. américaine   f. canadienne
   g. de Québec   h. de Montréal

2. a. un ami   b. un copain
   c. américain   d. canadien
   e. de Boston   f. de Baltimore
   g. Patrick   h. Paul

D. *Questions et réponses*

▶ — Elle est française?   — Comment s'appelle-t-elle?
  — **Oui, elle est française.**   — **Elle s'appelle Isabelle.**

▶ Isabelle

1. Marc

2. Philippe

3. Nathalie

4. Patrick

UNITÉ 2

CASSETTE WORKSHEET Leçon 6 (cont.)

Section 3 | **Les nombres de 80 à 100**

E. *Écoutez et répétez.*

80	81	82	83	84	85	86	87	88	89	
90	91	92	93	94	95	96	97	98	99	100

F. *Écoutez et écrivez.*

Florence	Juliette	Philippe	Laure

Delphine	Julien	Olivier	Caroline

Section 4 | **Prononciation**

G. *La voyelle nasale* /ɛ̃/

In French, there are three nasal vowel sounds.

Écoutez: **cinq onze trente**

Practice the sound /ɛ̃/ in the following words. Note that this vowel sound can have several different spellings.

➡ Be sure not to pronounce an "**n**" or "**m**" after the nasal vowel.

Répétez: "in"   ci**n**q qui**n**ze vi**ngt** vi**ngt**-ci**n**q
 quatre-vi**ngt**-qui**n**ze
"ain"   america**in** Ala**in** copa**in**
"(i)en" bie**n** canadie**n** tie**ns**!
"un"   u**n**
Tie**ns**! Voilà Ala**in**. Il est america**in**. Et Julie**n**?
 Il est canadie**n**.

Nom _______________________________

Classe _____________________________ Date ___________

CASSETTE WORKSHEET Leçon 7 Les photos d'Isabelle

Section 1 **Les photos d'Isabelle**

A. *Compréhension orale*

Isabelle is showing her family photo album to her friend Jean-Paul.

ISABELLE: Voici ma mère.
JEAN-PAUL: Et le monsieur, c'est ton père?
ISABELLE: Non, c'est mon oncle Thomas.
JEAN-PAUL: Et la fille, c'est ta cousine?
ISABELLE: Oui, c'est ma cousine Béatrice. Elle a seize ans.
JEAN-PAUL: Et le garçon, c'est ton cousin?
ISABELLE: Non, c'est un copain.
JEAN-PAUL: Un copain ou ton copain?
ISABELLE: Dis donc, Jean-Paul, tu es vraiment trop curieux!

B. *Écoutez et répétez.*

UNITÉ 2

CASSETTE WORKSHEET Leçon 7 (cont.)

Section 2 La famille d'Isabelle

C. *Compréhension orale*

a. _____ Papa
(mon père)

b. _1_ Maman
(ma mère)

c. _____ Papi
(mon grand-père)

d. _____ Mamie
(ma grand-mère)

e. _____ Nicolas
(mon frère)

f. _____ Valérie
(ma soeur)

g. _____ Médor
(mon chien)

h. _____ Félix
(mon chat)

i. _____ Oncle Thomas
(mon oncle)

j. _____ Tante Christine
(ma tante)

k. _____ Cédric
(mon cousin)

l. _____ Béatrice
(ma cousine)

CASSETTE WORKSHEET Leçon 7 (cont.)

Section 3 | **Quel âge as-tu?**

D. *Compréhension orale*

▶ Marc a __13__ ans.

1. Karen a _____ ans.

2. Pierre a _____ ans.

3. Jean-François a _____ ans.

4. Sylvie a _____ ans.

5. Annie a _____ ans.

6. Bernard a _____ ans.

E. *Compréhension orale*

1. Madame Galand a _____ ans.

2. Mademoiselle Rivière a _____ ans.

3. Monsieur Giraud a _____ ans.

4. Monsieur Pascal a _____ ans.

5. Madame Mercier a _____ ans.

UNITÉ 2

UNITÉ 2

CASSETTE WORKSHEET Leçon 7 (cont.)

F. *Questions et réponses*

Section 4 Prononciation

G. *Les voyelles nasales* /ã/ *et* /õ/

The letters "**an**" or "**en**" usually represent the nasal vowel /ã/. Be sure not to pronounce an "**n**" after the nasal vowel.

Répétez: ans tante grand-père français
anglais quarante cinquante
trente comment Henri Laurent

The letters "**on**" represent the nasal vowel /õ/. Be sure not to pronounce an "**n**" after the nasal vowel.

Répétez: non mon ton bonjour oncle
garçon onze

Contrastez: an—on tante—ton onze—ans
Mon oncle François a trente ans.

Nom _______________________________

Classe _________________________________ Date _______________

CASSETTE WORKSHEET Leçon 8 Le français pratique: Le jour et la date

| Section 1 | **Quel jour est-ce?** |

A. *Compréhension orale*

> *For many people, the days of the week are not all alike.*
>
> **Dialogue 1. Vendredi**
>
> PHILIPPE: Quel jour est-ce?
> STÉPHANIE: C'est vendredi!
> PHILIPPE: Super! Demain, c'est samedi!
>
> **Dialogue 2. Mercredi**
>
> NATHALIE: Ça va?
> MARC: Pas très bien.
> NATHALIE: Pourquoi?
> MARC: Aujourd'hui, c'est mercredi.
> NATHALIE: Et alors?
> MARC: Demain, c'est jeudi! Le jour de l'examen.
> NATHALIE: Zut! C'est vrai! Au revoir, Marc.
> MARC: Au revoir, Nathalie. À demain!

B. *Écoutez et répétez.*

| Section 2 | **Les jours de la semaine** |

C. *Écoutez et écrivez.*

▶ Christine arrive mardi.

▶ Christine

1. Pauline

2. Bertrand

3. Céline

4. Didier

5. Agnès

6. Guillaume

7. Véronique

| a. lundi |
| b. mardi |
| c. mercredi |
| d. jeudi |
| e. vendredi |
| f. samedi |
| g. dimanche |

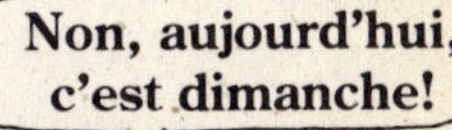

UNITÉ 2

CASSETTE WORKSHEET Leçon 8 (cont.)

Section 3 | Anniversaire

D. *Compréhension orale*

François wants to know when Isabelle's birthday is.

FRANÇOIS: C'est quand, ton anniversaire?
ISABELLE: C'est le 18 mars!
FRANÇOIS: Le 18 mars? Pas possible!
ISABELLE: Si! Pourquoi?
FRANÇOIS: C'est aussi mon anniversaire.
ISABELLE: Quelle coïncidence!

E. *Écoutez et répétez.*

Section 4 | Quel jour est-ce?

F. *Compréhension orale*

▶ C'est le ___2___ février.

1. C'est le ____ mars.

2. C'est le ____ juin.

3. C'est le ____ juillet.

4. C'est le ____ août.

5. C'est le ____ septembre.

6. C'est le ____ novembre.

CASSETTE WORKSHEET Leçon 8 (cont.)

G. *Questions et réponses*

▶ — Quel jour est-ce?
 — C'est le **5 décembre.**

▶ 

1.

2.

3.

4.

5.

6.

7.

Section 5   **C'est quand, votre anniversaire?**

H. *Compréhension orale*

▶ Alice: le __18/7__

1. Béatrice: le __________

2. Françoise: le __________

3. Julie: le __________

4. Delphine: le __________

5. Denis: le __________

6. Paul: le __________

UNITÉ 2

CASSETTE WORKSHEET Leçon 8 (cont.)

À votre tour!

Section 1. Nathalie et Philippe
 Allez à la page 52.

Section 2. Et toi?
 Allez à la page 52.

Section 3. Conversation dirigée
 Allez à la page 52.

Nom ____

Classe _________________________________ Date _______________

WRITING ACTIVITIES Leçon 5 Copain ou copine?

1. Pour détectives

You have found a notebook in which several people are mentioned
only by their initials. Read the descriptions and determine who is
male and who is female. Circle the corresponding letter.

▶ J.G. est un journaliste français. Ⓜ F
▶ C.C. est une actrice italienne. M Ⓕ
1. B.H. est un musicien anglais. M F
2. V.C. est un pianiste. M F
3. S.F. est une photographe américaine. M F
4. E.M. est une artiste française. M F
5. P.N. est un excellent acteur. M F
6. T.B. est un artiste américain. M F
7. P.V. est un cousin de San Francisco. M F
8. V.U. est une cousine de Montréal. M F

2. Descriptions

Describe the following people. For each one, write two sentences using two
different nouns from the box. Be sure to use **un** or **une** as appropriate.

garçon	**ami**	**copain**	**monsieur**	**prof**
fille	**amie**	**copine**	**dame**	**prof**

▶ C'est une fille. ______________________

Christine ______________________

Jean-François ______________________

M. Martinot ______________________

Mme Pichon ______________________

FLASH **culturel**

The **Tour de France** is an international bicycle race that is held in
France every summer. How long does it last?

☐ 10 hours   ☐ 24 hours   ☐ 10 days   ☐ 3 weeks

➡ **page 48**

UNITÉ 2

WRITING ACTIVITIES Leçon 5 (cont.)

3. Les nombres

Fill in the six missing numbers in the grid. Then write out these numbers in French.

60		62	63	64
65	66	67		69
		72	73	74
75		77		79

- _______________________________
- _______________________________
- _______________________________
- _______________________________
- _______________________________
- _______________________________

4. Communication: En français!

1. You are walking in town with your French friend Catherine. Catherine waves hello to a girl on a bicycle.

   Ask Catherine who it is.

   ____

2. You see Jean-Louis who is sitting in a café.

   Point him out and tell Catherine that he is a friend.

   ____

3. You see your friend Juliette coming in your direction.

   Express your surprise and explain to Catherine who is approaching.

   ____

FLASH culturel

The **Tour de France** is the longest and most strenuous bicycle race in the world. It is divided into about 20 stages (or **étapes**) and lasts approximately three weeks. During the race, the participants cover about 3,000 kilometers, riding along the valleys and climbing the high mountains of France. The American cyclist Greg Lemond is a three-time winner of the **Tour de France**.

Classe ___________________________ Date _______________

WRITING ACTIVITIES Leçon 6 Une coïncidence

1. *Le, la ou l'?*
Write **le, la,** or **l'** in front of the following nouns, as appropriate.

▶ <u>la</u>____ copine

1. ____ garçon   3. ____ fille   5. ____ copain   7. ____ prof: M. Lenoir
2. ____ monsieur   4. ____ ami   6. ____ amie   8. ____ prof: Mme Dupin

2. Photos de vacances
Last summer you went on an international camping trip and took pictures
of some of your friends. Give each person's name and nationality.

▶ Il s'appelle Jim.

Il est anglais.

____

____

____

____

____

____

FLASH culturel

In the United States, there are many places that have names of
French origin. Which of the following states is named after a
French king?

☐ Georgia   ☐ North Carolina   ☐ Louisiana   ☐ Virginia

➡ **page 50**

UNITÉ 2

WRITING ACTIVITIES Leçon 6 (cont.)

UNITÉ 2

3. Loto

Imagine that you are playing **Loto** in France. The following numbers have been called.
Read them carefully and put an "X" on the numbers that appear on your **Loto** card.

soixante-treize	soixante-quatre	quatorze	cinquante-trois	huit
quatre-vingt-douze	vingt-trois	quatre-vingt-neuf	soixante-quinze	
cinquante-huit	trente-sept	quarante-cinq	soixante-quatorze	seize
vingt et un	quatre-vingt-six	soixante-dix-huit	quatre-vingt-un	

Which row did you complete to
win **Loto:** the top, the middle, or
the bottom?

____

Now write in digits the numbers
that were not on your card.

____

		21		45			73	81	92
	17				53		74	86	95
8			39			64	78		99

4. À votre tour *(Your turn)*

Now it's your turn to call out the **Loto** numbers. Write out in French what you would say.

1. (95) ______________ 3. (27) ______________ 5. (79) ______________

2. (83) ______________ 4. (62) ______________ 6. (90) ______________

5. 🗣 Communication: Dialogues

Complete the following mini-dialogues by filling in the missing words.

1. —Philippe __________ français?   3. —__________ s'appelle __________ prof?

   —Non, __________ est canadien.   —__________ s'appelle Madame Vallée.

2. —Tu __________ le garçon là-bas?

   —Oui, c'est __________ copain.

FLASH culturel

Louisiana was named in honor of the French king Louis XIV
(1638–1715). Louisiana was once a French colony and extended
up the entire Mississippi basin. The U.S. purchased it from France
in 1803. Today, French is still spoken in the state of Louisiana by
some people in the "Cajun" areas.

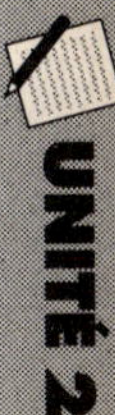

Nom ______________________________

Classe ______________________________ Date ______________

WRITING ACTIVITIES   Leçon 7   Les photos d'Isabelle

1. La famille de Catherine

Catherine has taken a picture of her family. Identify each of the people on the photograph.

▶ Suzanne est ______*la soeur*______ de Catherine.

1. M. Arnaud est ______________________ de Catherine.

2. Jean-Michel est ______________________ de Catherine.

3. Mme Laurent est ______________________ de Catherine.

4. Mme Arnaud est ______________________ de Catherine.

5. M. Laurent est ______________________ de Catherine.

6. Hugo, c'est ______________________ .

7. Mimi, c'est ______________________ .

FLASH culturel

At what age can a French teenager drive a car?

☐ 15   ☐ 16   ☐ 17   ☐ 18   ➜ **page 52**

WRITING ACTIVITIES Leçon 7 (cont.)

2. *Mon ou ma?*

Philippe is talking about his friends and relatives, as well as other people
he knows. Complete his statements with **mon** or **ma,** as appropriate.

1. _________ cousine s'appelle Christine.

2. _________ frère est à Paris.

3. _________ copine Susan est anglaise.

4. _________ amie Cécile a seize ans.

5. _________ ami Jean-Pierre a quinze ans.

6. _________ prof d'anglais est américaine.

7. _________ prof d'histoire est canadien.

8. _________ mère est journaliste.

3. Quel âge?

Look at the years in which the following people were born. Then
complete the sentences below by giving each person's age.

1. (1987) Corinne _________________________________ .

2. (1992) Jean-Philippe _________________________________ .

3. (1978) Mademoiselle Richaume _________________________ .

4. (1965) Monsieur Lambert _________________________________ .

4. Communication: En français!

1. *Tell how old you are.*

____

2. *Ask a friend how old he/she is.*

____

3. *Ask a friend how old his/her brother is.*

____

FLASH culturel

In principle, you have to be 18 to get your driver's license in
France. However, if you take driving lessons in an authorized
school **(une auto-école),** you can drive at the age of 16 when
accompanied by a licensed adult.

Nom ____

Classe _______________________________ Date _____________

UNITÉ 2

WRITING ACTIVITIES   Leçon 8 Le français pratique: Le jour et la date

1. La semaine

Can you fit the seven days of the week into the following French puzzle?

1. **S** □ □ □ □ □
2. □ **E** □ □ □
3. **M** □ □ □ □ □ □ □
4. □ **A** □ □ □
5. □ **I** □ □ □ □ □
6. □ □ **N** □ □
7. □ **E** □ □ □ □ □

2. Les mois

Complete the grid with the names of the missing months.

janvier		mars
avril	mai	
		septembre
octobre	novembre	

FLASH culturel

In France, **le quatorze juillet** is a very important date. What do the French do on that day?

☐ They vote.   ☐ They celebrate their national holiday.
☐ They pay their taxes.   ☐ They honor their war veterans.

➜ **page 54**

WRITING ACTIVITIES Leçon 8 (cont.)

3. Joyeux anniversaire! *(Happy birthday!)*

Ask five friends when their birthdays are. Write out the information in French on the chart below.

NOM	ANNIVERSAIRE
▶ David	le trois juillet
1.	
2.	
3.	
4.	
5.	

4. Communication: En français!

Answer the following questions in complete sentences.

1. Quel jour est-ce aujourd'hui?

____

2. Et demain?

____

3. Quelle est la date aujourd'hui?

____

4. C'est quand ton anniversaire?

____

𝓕LASH culturel

On July 14, or "Bastille Day" as it is known in the United States, the French celebrate their national holiday. On July 14, 1789, a Parisian mob stormed **la Bastille,** a state prison which had come to symbolize the king's tyranny. This important historical event marked the beginning of the French Revolution and led to the establishment of a republican form of government for the first time in French history.

Nom ______________________________

Classe __________________________   Date ____________

READING AND CULTURE ACTIVITIES Unité 2

A. En voyage

1. CEEL is a language school in Geneva. They teach four languages including German **(allemand)**, which is one of the official languages of Switzerland. Which of the following languages do they NOT teach?

☐ English.
☐ French.
☐ Spanish.
☐ Italian.

2. This brochure advertises a film festival in Montreal. When is the festival being held?

☐ Early spring.
☐ Early summer.
☐ Late summer.
☐ Late fall.

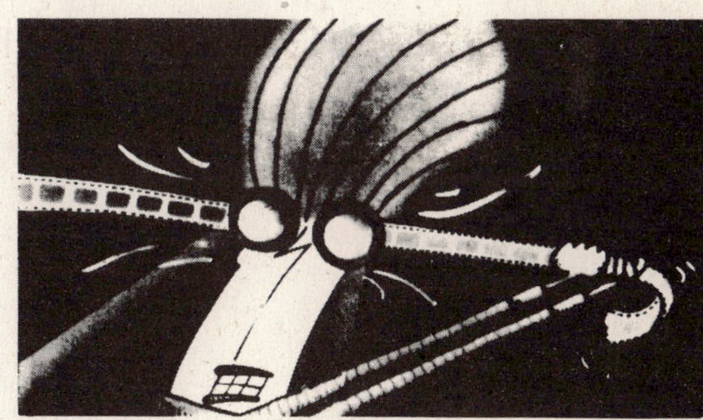

UNITÉ 2

READING AND CULTURE ACTIVITIES   Unité 2 (cont.)

3. This is a card of phone numbers that was distributed in Strasbourg, France.

- You would dial 15 if you had . . .
  - ☐ a medical emergency
  - ☐ a problem with your telephone
  - ☐ a fire to report
  - ☐ a burglary to report

- To get a prescription filled,
  you would call . . .
  - ☐ 15
  - ☐ 18
  - ☐ 03.88.41.12.45
  - ☐ 03.88.61.54.13

- If you needed transportation to get
  to the airport, you would call . . .
  - ☐ 15
  - ☐ 18
  - ☐ 88.41.12.45
  - ☐ 88.61.54.13

NUMÉROS D'URGENCE		
	SAMU (Service d'Aide Médicale d'Urgence)	15
	POLICE	17
	POMPIERS	18
	PHARMACIE	03.88.41.12.45
	TAXIS	03.88.61.54.13

4. The following flyer was distributed in Paris.

- What does this flyer advertise?
  - ☐ A play.
  - ☐ A concert.
  - ☐ A piano recital.
  - ☐ A ballet.

- How many performances will there be?
  - ☐ 5
  - ☐ 8
  - ☐ 15
  - ☐ 50

- When is the last performance?
  - ☐ January 1.
  - ☐ June 1.
  - ☐ July 14.
  - ☐ November 8.

READING AND CULTURE ACTIVITIES   Unité 2 (cont.)

B. Les boutiques du Palais des Congrès

In this ad, the shops at the Paris Convention Center (**le Palais des Congrès**) are announcing a large sale. Look at the ad carefully.

- What is the French word for *sale?*

  ____

- On what day does the sale begin?

  ____

- On what day does the sale end?

  ____

- Is there parking available? ___________

  For how many cars? ___________

C. «Un bon patriote»

Look at this Paris ticket for "Un bon patriote."

- Where is the performance being held?

  ____

- How much does the ticket cost?

  ____

- What is the date on the ticket?

  ____

- What day of the week is the performance?

  ____

- What time does the performance begin?

  ____

UNITÉ 2

READING AND CULTURE ACTIVITIES   **Unité 2** (cont.)

D. Une carte

Jean-Claude bought this card and has just signed it.

• To whom is he planning to send it?

____

• What is the special occasion?

____

UNITÉ 2

COMMUNICATIVE EXPRESSIONS AND THEMATIC VOCABULARY

Unité 2 Les copains et la famille

▶ CULTURAL CONTEXT: **Talking about people**

COMMUNICATIVE EXPRESSIONS

Introducing or pointing someone out
    Voici . . .   **Voilà . . .**

Inquiring about people and mentioning their nationality

Tu connais . . . ?	**Il est [français].** **Elle est [française].**
Qui est-ce? **C'est . . .**	

Asking about someone's name and age

Comment s'appelle . . . ?
  Il/Elle s'appelle . . .
	Quel âge as-tu?
	  J'ai [14] ans.

	Quel âge a . . . ? **Il/Elle a [15] ans.**

Talking about days, dates, and birthdays

Quel jour est-ce?
  C'est [mardi].
	Quelle est la date?
	  C'est le [10 novembre].
	  C'est le premier [mai].

	C'est quand, ton anniversaire? **C'est le [2 juillet].**

. . . .

VOCABULARY

People, family members, pets

un garçon	une fille	un frère	une soeur	un chat
un ami	une amie	un cousin	une cousine	un chien
un copain	une copine			
		un père	une mère	
un monsieur	une dame	un oncle	une tante	
un prof	une prof	un grand-père	une grand-mère	

COMMUNICATIVE EXPRESSIONS AND THEMATIC VOCABULARY

VOCABULARY (*continued*)

Days and months

un jour	un mois	

aujourd'hui
demain

un jour	un mois	
lundi	janvier	juillet
mardi	février	août
mercredi	mars	septembre
jeudi	avril	octobre
vendredi	mai	novembre
samedi	juin	décembre
dimanche		

Numbers: 60–100

soixante	soixante-dix	quatre-vingts	quatre-vingt-dix	cent
soixante et un	soixante et onze	quatre-vingt-un	quatre-vingt-onze	
soixante-deux	soixante-douze	quatre-vingt-deux	quatre-vingt-douze	
soixante-trois	soixante-treize	quatre-vingt-trois	quatre-vingt-treize	
soixante-quatre	soixante-quatorze	quatre-vingt-quatre	quatre-vingt-quatorze	
soixante-cinq	soixante-quinze	quatre-vingt-cinq	quatre-vingt-quinze	
soixante-six	soixante-seize	quatre-vingt-six	quatre-vingt-seize	
soixante-sept	soixante-dix-sept	quatre-vingt-sept	quatre-vingt-dix-sept	
soixante-huit	soixante-dix-huit	quatre-vingt-huit	quatre-vingt-dix-huit	
soixante-neuf	soixante-dix-neuf	quatre-vingt-neuf	quatre-vingt-dix-neuf	

Other expressions

un, une	tiens!
le, la, l'	à demain!
mon, ma	à samedi!
ton, ta	

UNITÉ 3
Bon appétit!

LISTENING ACTIVITIES
Leçons 9–12

WRITING ACTIVITIES
Leçons 9–12

READING AND CULTURE ACTIVITIES
Unité 3

Communicative Expressions and Thematic Vocabulary

Nom _______________________________

Classe _____________________________ Date ____________

CASSETTE WORKSHEET Leçon 9 Tu as faim?

Section 1 Tu as faim?

A. *Compréhension orale*

> *Pierre, Philippe, and Nathalie are on their way home from school. They stop to get something to eat. Today it is Pierre's turn to treat his friends.*
>
> **Scène 1. Pierre et Nathalie**
>
> PIERRE: Tu as faim?
> NATHALIE: Oui, j'ai faim.
> PIERRE: Qu'est-ce que tu veux, un sandwich ou une pizza?
> NATHALIE: Donne-moi une pizza, s'il te plaît.
> PIERRE: Voilà.
> NATHALIE: Merci.
>
> **Scène 2. Pierre et Philippe**
>
> PIERRE: Et toi, Philippe, tu as faim?
> PHILIPPE: Oh là, là, oui, j'ai faim.
> PIERRE: Qu'est-ce que tu veux, un sandwich ou une pizza?
> PHILIPPE: Je voudrais un sandwich . . . euh . . . et donne-moi aussi une pizza.
> PIERRE: C'est vrai! Tu as vraiment faim!

B. *Écoutez et répétez.*

Section 2 Je voudrais . . .

C. *Compréhension orale*

a. _____ trois croissants

b. _____ une glace à la vanille

c. _____ un hot dog

d. __1__ un sandwich

e. _____ un sandwich au jambon et un sandwich au pâté

f. _____ un steak-frites et une salade

D. *Compréhension orale*

a. _____ l'Express

b. _____ 20 euros

c. _____ un album d'Astérix

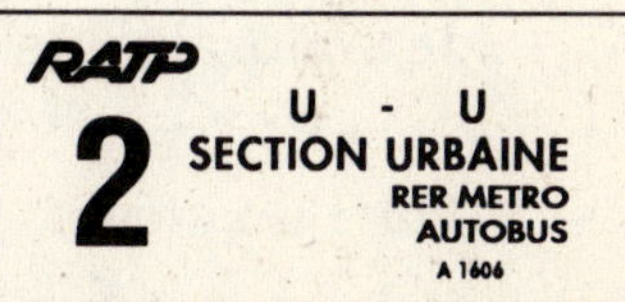

d. _____ un ticket de métro

CASSETTE WORKSHEET Leçon 9 (cont.)

Section 3 | **Au café**

E. *Questions et réponses*

▶ —Tu veux un sandwich ou une pizza?
  —**Je voudrais un sandwich.**

▶

1.   **2.**   **3.**   **4.**   **5.**

Section 4 | **Prononciation**

F. *L'intonation*

Écoutez: **Voici un steak . . . et une salade.**

When you speak, your voice rises and falls. This is called INTONATION. In French, as in English, your voice goes down at the end of a statement. However, in French, your voice rises after each group of words in the middle of a sentence. (This is the opposite of English, where your voice drops a little when you pause in the middle of a sentence.)

Répétez: **Je voudrais une pizza.**

Je voudrais une pizza et un sandwich.

Je voudrais une pizza, un sandwich et un hamburger.

Voici un steak.

Voici un steak et une salade.

Nom _______________________________

Classe _____________________________ Date _______________

CASSETTE WORKSHEET Leçon 10 Au café

| Section 1 | **Au café** |

A. *Compréhension orale*

Jean-Paul and Isabelle are tired and thirsty after an afternoon of shopping. Jean-Paul invites Isabelle to a café.

Scène 1

JEAN-PAUL: Tu as soif?

ISABELLE: Oui, j'ai soif.

JEAN-PAUL: On va dans un café? Je t'invite.

ISABELLE: D'accord!

Scène 2

LE GARÇON: Vous désirez, mademoiselle?

ISABELLE: Un jus d'orange, s'il vous plaît.

LE GARÇON: Et vous, monsieur?

JEAN-PAUL: Hmmm . . . Donnez-moi une limonade, s'il vous plaît.

Scène 3

LE GARÇON: La limonade, c'est pour vous, mademoiselle?

JEAN-PAUL: Non, c'est pour moi.

LE GARÇON: Ah, excusez-moi. Voici le jus d'orange, mademoiselle.

ISABELLE: Merci.

B. *Écoutez et répétez.*

CASSETTE WORKSHEET Leçon 10 (cont.)

Section 2 *S'il vous plaît ou s'il te plaît?*

C. *Compréhension orale*

How to say *please:*

Formal form: **s'il vous plaît**

ISABELLE: Un jus d'orange, s'il vous plaît.
JEAN-PAUL: Donnez-moi une limonade, s'il vous plaît.

Informal form: **s'il te plaît**

JEAN-PAUL: Donne-moi un soda, s'il te plaît.

D. *Écoutez et écrivez.*

1

a. ____ s'il vous plaît
b. ____ s'il te plaît

6

a. ____ s'il vous plaît
b. ____ s'il te plaît

2
a. ____ s'il vous plaît
b. ____ s'il te plaît

7
a. ____ s'il vous plaît
b. ____ s'il te plaît

3
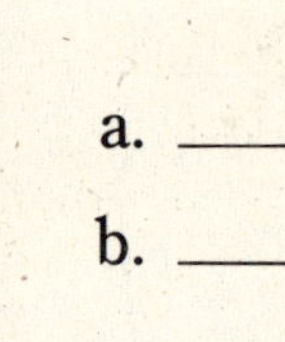
a. ____ s'il vous plaît
b. ____ s'il te plaît

8

a. ____ s'il vous plaît
b. ____ s'il te plaît

4

a. ____ s'il vous plaît
b. ____ s'il te plaît

9

a. ____ s'il vous plaît
b. ____ s'il te plaît

5
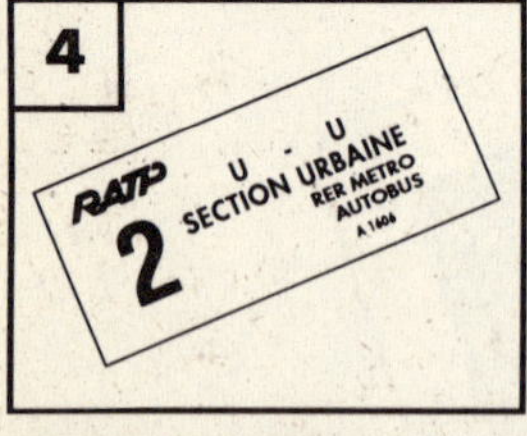
a. ____ s'il vous plaît
b. ____ s'il te plaît

10

a. ____ s'il vous plaît
b. ____ s'il te plaît

CASSETTE WORKSHEET Leçon 10 (cont.)

Section 3 S'il te plaît, donne-moi . . .

E. *Questions et réponses*

▶ —Tu veux un café ou un thé?
—S'il te plaît, donne-moi un café.

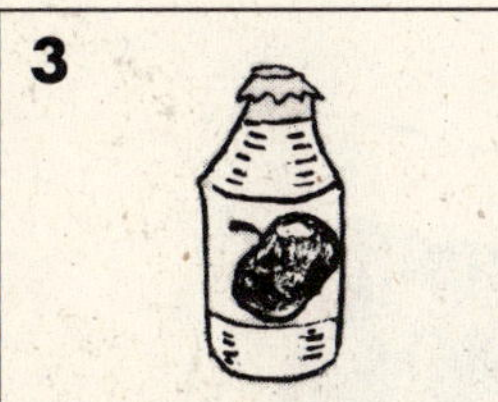

Section 4 Vous désirez?

F. *Questions et réponses*

▶ —Vous désirez?
—Je voudrais un thé, s'il vous plaît.

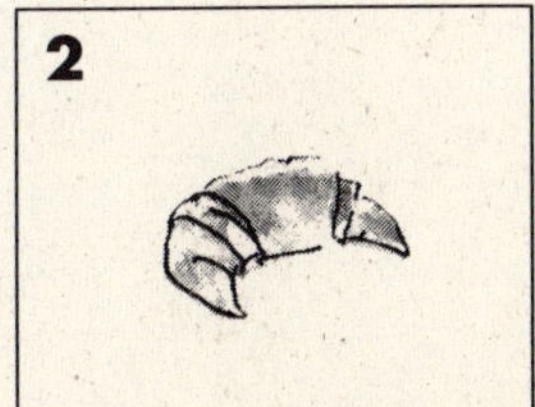
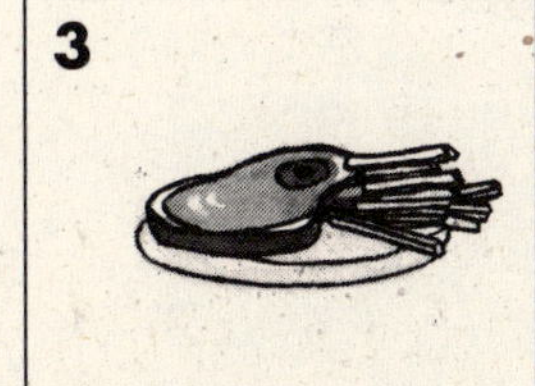

CASSETTE WORKSHEET . Leçon 10 (cont.)

Section 5 | **Prononciation**

G. *L'accent final*

Écoutez: **un choco<u>lat</u>**

In French, the rhythm is very even and the accent always falls on the *last* syllable of a word or group of words.

Répétez: **Phi<u>li</u>ppe   Tho<u>mas</u>   A<u>lice</u>   So<u>phie</u>   Domi<u>nique</u>**
   un ca<u>fé</u> Je voudrais un ca<u>fé</u>.
   une sa<u>lade</u> Donnez-moi une sa<u>lade</u>.
   un choco<u>lat</u> Donne-moi un choco<u>lat</u>.

UNITÉ 3

CASSETTE WORKSHEET Leçon 11 Ça fait combien?

Section 1 | Ça fait combien?

A. *Compréhension orale*

> *At the café, Jean-Paul and Isabelle are ready to leave. Jean-Paul calls the waiter so he can pay the check.*
>
> JEAN-PAUL: S'il vous plaît?
> LE GARÇON: Oui, monsieur.
> JEAN-PAUL: Ça fait combien?
> LE GARÇON: Voyons, un jus d'orange, 2 euros, et une limonade, 1 euro. Ça fait 3 euros.
> JEAN-PAUL: 3 euros . . .Très bien . . .Zut! Où est mon porte-monnaie . . .? Dis, Isabelle, prête-moi 5 euros, s'il te plaît.

B. *Écoutez et répétez.*

Section 2 | C'est combien?

C. *Compréhension orale*

▶ __60__ euros

1. _____ euros

2. _____ euros

3. _____ euros

4. _____ euros

5. _____ euros

CASSETTE WORKSHEET Leçon 11 (cont.)

| Section 3 | Au café |

D. *Questions et réponses*

1.

2.

3.

4.

| Section 4 | Prononciation |

E. *La consonne "r"*

Écoutez: **Ma_r_ie**

The French consonant "**r**" is not at all like the English "**r**". It is pronounced at the back of the throat. In fact, it is similar to the Spanish "jota" sound of _J_osé.

Répétez: **Ma_r_ie Pa_r_is o_r_ange Hen_r_i
_fr_anc t_r_ès c_r_oissant _fr_omage
bonjou_r_ pou_r_ Pie_rr_e qua_r_t
_R_obe_r_t _R_ichard _R_enée _R_aoul
Ma_r_ie, p_r_ête-moi t_r_ente f_r_ancs.**

Nom ____

Classe _________________________________ Date _____________

CASSETTE WORKSHEET Leçon 12 Le français pratique: Le temps

Section 1 Le temps

A. *Compréhension orale*

It is nine o'clock Sunday morning. Cécile and her brother Philippe have planned a picnic for the whole family. Cécile is asking about the weather.

CÉCILE: Quel temps fait-il?
PHILIPPE: Il fait mauvais!
CÉCILE: Il fait mauvais?
PHILIPPE: Oui, il fait mauvais! Regarde! Il pleut!
CÉCILE: Oh, zut, zut et zut!
PHILIPPE: !!!???
CÉCILE: Et le pique-nique?
PHILIPPE: Le pique-nique? Ah, oui, le pique-nique! . . . Écoute, ça n'a pas d'importance.
CÉCILE: Pourquoi?
PHILIPPE: Pourquoi? Parce que Papa va nous inviter au restaurant.
CÉCILE: Super!

B. *Écoutez et répétez.*

Section 2 Quel temps fait-il?

C. *Compréhension orale*

1.   2.   3.   4.   5.   6.   7.   8.

a. Il fait frais.

h. Il fait froid.

b. Il fait bon.

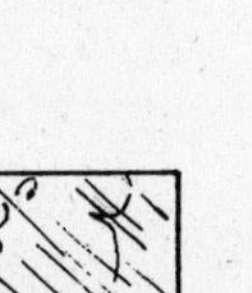
f. Il pleut.

g. Il fait mauvais.

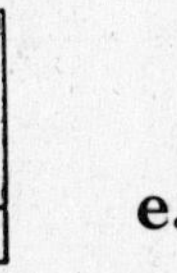
c. Il fait chaud.

d. Il fait beau.

e. Il neige.

CASSETTE WORKSHEET   Leçon 12   (cont.)

D. *Questions et réponses*

À votre tour!

Section 1. Isabelle et Jean-Paul

Allez à la page 72.

Section 2. Et toi?

Allez à la page 72.

Section 3. Conversation dirigée

Allez à la page 72.

WRITING ACTIVITIES Leçon 9 Tu as faim?

1. *Un* ou *une*?

Complete the names of the following foods with **un** or **une,** as appropriate.

 1. __________ sandwich

 5. __________ steak-frites

 2. __________ pizza

 6. __________ salade

 3. __________ steak

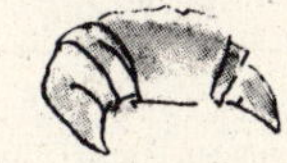 7. __________ croissant

 4. __________ crêpe

 8. __________ omelette

2. Conversations

Complete the conversations with expressions from the box.

1. —Tu as faim?

   —Oui, _____________ faim.

2. —Qu'est-ce que _________________ ?

   —Je _________________ une glace.

3. —S'il te plaît, _____________ un sandwich.

   —Voilà un sandwich.

   — _____________ !

> merci
> tu veux
> j'ai
> je voudrais
> donne-moi

FLASH culturel

Camembert, brie, and roquefort are all products of French origin.
What are they?

☐ pastries   ☐ cheeses   ☐ perfumes   ☐ crackers   → page 74

UNITÉ 3

WRITING ACTIVITIES Leçon 9 (cont.)

3.  Communication: En français!

A. You have invited your French friend Philippe to your home.

1. *Ask Philippe if he is hungry.*

____

2. *Ask him if he wants a sandwich.*

____

3. *Ask him if he wants an ice cream cone.*

____

B. You are in a French restaurant with a friend.

1. *Tell your friend that you are hungry.*

____

2. *Tell her what type of food you would like to have.*

____

FLASH culturel

France produces over 400 varieties of cheese, among which **camembert, brie,** and **roquefort** are the best known. In a traditional French meal, cheese is served as a separate course, after the salad and before the dessert. It is eaten with bread, and occasionally with butter.

WRITING ACTIVITIES Leçon 10 Au café

1. Les boissons

Find the French names of eight beverages in the following grid. The names can be read horizontally, vertically, or diagonally. Then list these beverages, using **un** or **une,** as appropriate.

J	O	J	B	M	N	C	I	X	Y	A	Z
M	U	U	R	E	W	H	L	Q	B	C	F
J	U	S	D	E	T	O	M	A	T	E	R
K	V	D	D	L	G	C	C	U	K	N	Z
X	D	E	A	E	L	O	H	T	L	Z	C
Y	B	P	A	F	R	L	C	H	X	T	P
Z	S	O	D	A	C	A	F	É	J	M	B
O	N	M	C	K	B	T	I	N	K	A	Y
L	I	M	O	N	A	D	E	S	D	O	C
S	Q	E	T	F	I	P	D	V	I	G	L
H	T	W	M	R	O	S	Y	I	U	N	J

- ______________________
- ______________________
- ______________________
- ______________________
- ______________________
- ______________________
- ______________________
- ______________________

2. Mes préférences

In the chart below, list which three of the above beverages you like the best and which three you like the least.

1. _______________________   4. _______________________

2. _______________________   5. _______________________

3. _______________________   6. _______________________

FLASH culturel

Which of the following beverages is most likely to be served with a French meal?

☐ milk   ☐ coffee   ☐ iced tea   ☐ mineral water

➡ **page 76**

WRITING ACTIVITIES Leçon 10 (cont.)

3. Communication: En français!

A. Your French friend Marc has dropped by your house.

1. *Ask him if he is thirsty.*

____

2. *Ask him if he wants a soda or a glass of orange juice.*

____

B. You are in a French café with a friend.

1. *Tell your friend that you are thirsty.*

____

2. *Tell the waiter (or waitress) to bring you a beverage of your choice.*

____

*F*LASH **culturel**

The French drink a lot of mineral water. In fact, they have the highest consumption of mineral water in the world: about 60 liters per person per year. These mineral waters, some plain and some carbonated, come from natural springs in various parts of the country and are widely exported. The best known are Évian, Vittel, Perrier, and Vichy.

WRITING ACTIVITIES Leçon 11 Ça fait combien?

1. C'est combien?
Identify the items pictured and give their prices.

▶ 
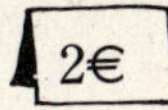

Voici un sandwich. _______________________

Il coûte deux euros . _______________________

1.  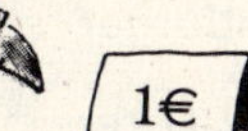
____
____

2. 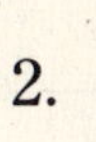 
____
____

3. 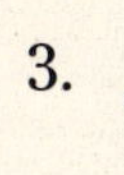 
____
____

4. 
____
____

5. 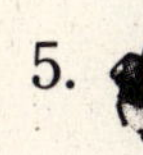 
____
____

6. 
____
____

FLASH culturel

The backs of the euro bills are illustrated with pictures of bridges. Which bill has the most modern bridge?

☐ 10 euro note ☐ 50 euro note ☐ 100 euro note ☐ 500 euro note

→ page 78

UNITÉ 3

WRITING ACTIVITIES Leçon 11 (cont.)

2. Communication: En français!

Imagine that you are at Le Rallye with two French friends, Olivier and Valérie.

Use the menu to write out the following conversation (in French, of course!).

<table>
<tr><td colspan="2">Le Rallye</td></tr>
<tr><td colspan="2">Boissons</td><td colspan="2">Sandwichs</td></tr>
<tr><td>Café</td><td>2€</td><td>Sandwich au jambon</td><td>3€50</td></tr>
<tr><td>Thé</td><td>2€</td><td>Sandwich au fromage</td><td>3€50</td></tr>
<tr><td>Chocolat</td><td>2€50</td><td colspan="2">Et aussi:</td></tr>
<tr><td>Soda</td><td>2€50</td><td>Croissant</td><td>2€</td></tr>
<tr><td>Limonade</td><td>2€25</td><td>Pizza</td><td>3€</td></tr>
<tr><td>Jus d'orange</td><td>2€50</td><td>Salade</td><td>2€50</td></tr>
<tr><td>Eau minérale</td><td>1€50</td><td>Omelette</td><td>3€50</td></tr>
<tr><td colspan="2">Glaces</td><td>Hamburger</td><td>4€</td></tr>
<tr><td>Glace au café</td><td>2€50</td><td>Steak</td><td>5€50</td></tr>
<tr><td>Glace à la vanille</td><td>2€50</td><td>Steak-Frites</td><td>6€50</td></tr>
</table>

LE GARÇON: _______________________________

May I help you?

TOI: _______________________________

I would like [a food and a beverage].

VALÉRIE: _______________________________

Please give me [a food and a beverage].

OLIVIER: _______________________________

I would like [a food and a beverage], please.

TOI: _______________________________

How much does that come to?

LE GARÇON: _______________________________

That comes to [the price of what was ordered].

TOI: _______________________________

Hey, Olivier, loan me ten euros, please.

*F*LASH culturel

The bills are sequenced so that the styles of bridges go from the oldest (5 euro note) to the most modern (500 euro note).

The 500 € bill

UNITÉ 3

Nom ____

Classe _____________________________ Date ___________

WRITING ACTIVITIES Leçon 12   Le français pratique: Le temps

1. Les quatre saisons

Write the names of the seasons associated with the following pictures.

__________   __________   __________   __________

2. La météo *(Weather report)*

Look at the map of France and describe the weather in the cities indicated below.

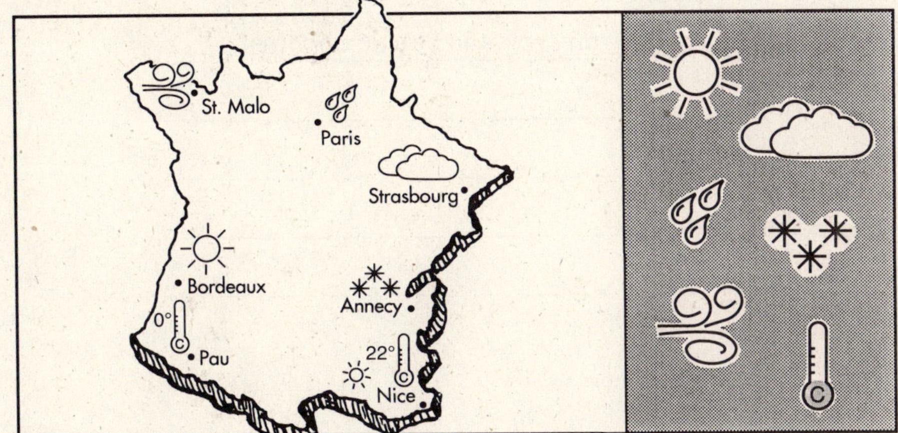

1. À Pau, ___________________________.   5. À Annecy, ___________________________.

2. À Nice, ___________________________.   6. À Saint Malo, ___________________________.

3. À Bordeaux, ___________________________.   7. À Paris, ___________________________.

4. À Strasbourg, ___________________________.

FLASH culturel

If you went to France for Christmas vacation, what kind of weather
should you expect?

☐ rain   ☐ snow   ☐ cold weather   ☐ mild weather   **➜ page 80**

WRITING ACTIVITIES Leçon 12 (cont.)

3. Communication: Quel temps fait-il?

Describe the weather in the city where you live.

1. Aujourd'hui, _________________________________ .

2. En été, _________________________________ .

3. En automne, _________________________________ .

4. En hiver, _________________________________ .

5. Au printemps, _________________________________ .

4. Communication: As-tu faim? As-tu soif?

When we go to a café, what we order often depends on the weather. Read each of the weather descriptions and then indicate what you would like to eat and/or drink.

Le Temps	**Au Café**
	S'il vous plaît, . . .
▶ Il fait froid.	donnez-moi _un croissant et un chocolat_ .
1. Il fait chaud.	donnez-moi _________________________ .
2. Il pleut.	donnez-moi _________________________ .
3. Il neige.	donnez-moi _________________________ .
4. Il fait frais.	donnez-moi _________________________ .

FLASH culturel

Since France is very geographically diverse, winter weather varies from region to region. It may snow and be quite cold in the Alps, the Pyrenees, and the mountains of central France. The weather may be rather mild along the Mediterranean and in southern France. In the rest of the country it may be cool and sometimes rainy.

UNITÉ 3

READING AND CULTURE ACTIVITIES Unité 3

A. Le petit déjeuner

Read the breakfast request that
Monsieur Chardon hung on the
doorknob of his hotel room.

1. When does M. Chardon want his
breakfast served?
☐ Before 7 A.M.
☐ Around 7:15 A.M.
☐ Around 7:45 A.M.
☐ He does not say.

2. What kind of juice is he ordering?
☐ Orange juice.
☐ Grapefruit juice.
☐ Apple juice.
☐ Tomato juice.

3. What does he want to eat?
☐ Toast.
☐ A muffin.
☐ A croissant.
☐ A Danish pastry.

4. What hot beverage is he ordering?
☐ Coffee.
☐ Hot chocolate.
☐ Tea with lemon.
☐ Tea with milk.

READING AND CULTURE ACTIVITIES Unité 3 (cont.)

B. La météo

La météo en bref:
23 janvier

Dans le nord de la France
il fait assez froid.

Dans la région parisienne,
il pleut.

Dans les Alpes, il neige.

Cependant sur la Côte d'Azur,
à Nice et à Cannes, il fait
beau temps.

1. What is the weather like in Paris?
- ☐ It's sunny.
- ☐ It's windy.
- ☐ It's rainy.
- ☐ It's snowing.

2. What is the weather like in the Alps?
- ☐ It's sunny.
- ☐ It's windy.
- ☐ It's rainy.
- ☐ It's snowing.

3. What is the weather like in Nice?
- ☐ It's sunny.
- ☐ It's windy.
- ☐ It's rainy.
- ☐ It's snowing.

READING AND CULTURE ACTIVITIES Unité 3 (cont.)

C. À la Terrasse Mailloux

The Terrasse Mailloux is a restaurant in Quebec City. This morning
you visited the Citadelle with a classmate, and now you have stopped
at the Terrasse Mailloux for lunch.

Together with your classmate, read the menu carefully and select
three dishes that you will each have.

- Write down the dishes you have selected.

- Then enter the prices for what you have chosen and total up each bill.

<table>
<tr><td colspan="2" align="center">MOI</td><td colspan="2" align="center">MON COPAIN/MA COPINE</td></tr>
<tr><td>PLAT</td><td>PRIX</td><td>PLAT</td><td>PRIX</td></tr>
<tr><td>________</td><td>______</td><td>________</td><td>______</td></tr>
<tr><td>________</td><td>______</td><td>________</td><td>______</td></tr>
<tr><td>________</td><td>______</td><td>________</td><td>______</td></tr>
<tr><td>TOTAL</td><td>______</td><td>TOTAL</td><td>______</td></tr>
</table>

UNITÉ 3

Terrasse Mailloux

entrées

Frites (French fries)	0.80
Frites avec sauce hot chicken	1.00
(French fries with hot chicken sauce)	
Frites avec sauce spaghetti	1.65
(French fries with spaghetti sauce)	
Oignons français (Onion rings)	1.50

salades

Au poulet (Chicken)	3.95
Au homard (en saison)	9.50
Lobster (in season)	
Salade du chef (Chef's salad)	1.50

pizza 9''

Fromage (Cheese)	3.25
Pepperoni	3.75
Garnie (All dressed)	4.25

sandwichs
(servis avec frites et salade de choux)
(served with French fries and cole slaw)

Salade aux oeufs (Egg salad)	2.00
Jambon (Ham)	2.50
Poulet (Chicken)	2.25
Tomates et bacon (Tomato & bacon)	2.50
Croque Monsieur	3.25

desserts

Salade de fruits (Fruit salad)	1.25
Tartes (Pies)	1.00
Gâteau moka (Mocha cake)	1.50
Gâteau Forêt Noire (Black Forest cake)	1.75

COMMUNICATIVE EXPRESSIONS AND THEMATIC VOCABULARY
Unité 3 Bon appétit!

▶ CULTURAL CONTEXT: **Having a snack in France**

COMMUNICATIVE EXPRESSIONS

Saying that you are hungry or thirsty
J'ai faim.	**J'ai soif.**
Tu as faim?	**Tu as soif?**

Offering a friend something
Tu veux . . . ?
Qu'est-ce que tu veux?

Asking a friend for something
Je voudrais . . .	**s'il te plaît**
Donne-moi . . .	
Prête-moi . . .	

Ordering in a café
Vous désirez?
   Je voudrais . . .   **s'il vous plaît**

Asking how much something costs
C'est combien?
Ça fait combien?
   Ça fait [50 euros, 20 centimes].

Combien coûte [un sandwich/une pizza]?
   Il/Elle coûte . . .

Talking about the weather
Quel temps fait-il?

Il fait	beau.	**Il neige.**
	bon	**Il pleut.**
	chaud	
	frais	
	froid	
	mauvais	

COMMUNICATIVE EXPRESSIONS AND THEMATIC VOCABULARY

VOCABULARY

Foods you can order in a café

un croissant	une crêpe
un hamburger	une glace
un hot dog	une omelette
un sandwich	une pizza
un steak	une salade
un steak-frites	

Beverages you can order in a café

un café	une limonade
un chocolat	
un thé	

un jus d'orange
un jus de pomme
un jus de raisin
un jus de tomate
un soda

The seasons

l'automne	en automne
l'été	en été
l'hiver	en hiver
le printemps	au printemps

UNITÉ 4
Qu'est-ce qu'on fait?

LISTENING ACTIVITIES
Leçons 13–16

WRITING ACTIVITIES
Leçons 13–16

READING AND CULTURE ACTIVITIES
Unité 4

Communicative Expressions and Thematic Vocabulary

Nom _______________________________

Classe ___________________________ Date ______________

CASSETTE WORKSHEET Leçon 13 Le français pratique: Mes activités

| Section 1 | **Préférences** |

A. *Écoutez et répétez.*

Allez à la page 90.

| Section 2 | **J'aime téléphoner** |

B. *Compréhension orale*

a. _____ danser

b. _____ écouter la musique

c. _____ jouer au tennis

d. _____ jouer au volley

e. _____ manger

f. _____ nager

g. _____ parler anglais

h. _____ regarder la télé

i. _1_ téléphoner

j. _____ voyager

UNITÉ 4

CASSETTE WORKSHEET   Leçon 13   (cont.)

Section 3   **Tu aimes écouter la radio?**

C. *Questions et réponses*

▶ —Tu aimes écouter la radio?
—**Oui, j'aime écouter la radio.**
(Non, je n'aime pas écouter la radio.)

CASSETTE WORKSHEET Leçon 13 (cont.)

D. *Questions*

▶ — Quelle est la question?
— **Tu aimes écouter la radio?**

▶ 

1.

2.

3.

4.

5.

6.

7.

Section 4	Invitations

E. *Compréhension orale*

1. At a party.   a. ____ accepts   b. ____ declines
2. By the tennis courts. a. ____ accepts   b. ____ declines
3. At home.   a. ____ accepts   b. ____ declines

CASSETTE WORKSHEET **Leçon 13** (cont.)

| **Section 5** | **Dialogue: Tennis?** |

F. *Écoutez et écrivez.*

1. Quelle est la question de Nicolas?

«Est-ce que tu _______________________________ avec moi?»

2. Quelle est la réponse de Jean-Claude?

«Je _____________ , mais je _______________________________ .»

3. Quelle est la réponse de Nathalie?

«Je _____________ , mais je _______________________________ .»

4. Quelle est la réponse de Marie?

«_______________________________ .»

5. À quelle heure est le match de tennis?

«À _______________________________ .»

À votre tour!

Section 6. Créa-dialogue

▶ Est-ce que tu veux jouer
au tennis avec moi?

1. Est-ce que tu veux jouer au basket avec moi?
2. Est-ce que tu veux manger une pizza?
3. Est-ce que tu veux regarder la télé?
4. Est-ce que tu veux jouer au ping-pong?
5. Est-ce que tu veux dîner au restaurant?

EXCUSES:

a. Je dois étudier.
b. Je dois travailler.
c. Je dois téléphoner à une copine.
d. Je dois dîner avec ma cousine.
e. Je dois parler avec ma mère.
f. Je dois chanter avec la chorale.

Section 7. Conversation dirigée

 Allez à la page 95.

UNITÉ 4

Nom ____

Classe ________________________________ Date ____________

CASSETTE WORKSHEET Leçon 14 Qui est là?

| Section 1 | **Qui est là?** |

A. *Compréhension orale*

> *It is Wednesday afternoon. Pierre is looking for his friends but cannot find anyone.*
> *Finally he sees Hélène at the Café Bellevue and asks her where everyone is.*
>
> PIERRE: Où est Jacqueline?
> HÉLÈNE: Elle est à la maison.
> PIERRE: Et Jean-Claude? Il est là?
> HÉLÈNE: Non, il n'est pas là.
> PIERRE: Où est-il?
> HÉLÈNE: Il est en ville avec une copine.
> PIERRE: Et Nicole et Sandrine? Est-ce qu'elles sont ici?
> HÉLÈNE: Non, elles sont au restaurant.
> PIERRE: Alors, qui est là?
> HÉLÈNE: Moi, je suis ici.
> PIERRE: C'est vrai, tu es ici! Eh bien, puisque tu es là, je t'invite au cinéma. D'accord?
> HÉLÈNE: Super! Pierre, tu es un vrai copain!

B. *Écoutez et répétez.*

| Section 2 | **Où es-tu?** |

C. *Compréhension orale*

Je suis . . .

	A	B	C	D
	au café	au cinéma	en classe	à la maison
▶		✓		
1				
2				
3				
4				
5				

UNITÉ 4

CASSETTE WORKSHEET Leçon 14 (cont.)

| Section 3 | Où êtes-vous? |

D. *Compréhension orale*

Nous sommes . . .

	A	B	C	D	E
	en classe	à Paris	en ville	en vacances	en France
▶				✓	
1					
2					
3					
4					
5					

UNITÉ 4

| Section 4 | Où sont-ils? |

E. *Questions et réponses*

▶ —Est-ce qu'il est à la maison ou au restaurant?
—**Il est au restaurant.**

CASSETTE WORKSHEET Leçon 14 (cont.)

| **Section 5** | **Dialogue: Où est Jean-Claude?** |

F. *Compréhension orale*

Frédéric sees his friend Nathalie on the way home from school.

FRÉDÉRIC: Salut!
NATHALIE: Salut, Frédéric!

FRÉDÉRIC: Jean-Claude ________________ avec toi?
NATHALIE: Non, il est avec Sandrine.

FRÉDÉRIC: ________________?

NATHALIE: Ils sont ________________ de l'Univers.

FRÉDÉRIC: ________________ Nathalie, salut!
NATHALIE: Salut!

FRÉDÉRIC: Salut, Sandrine!
SANDRINE: Salut, ça va?

FRÉDÉRIC: Oui, ça va. Jean-Claude n'est pas ________________?
SANDRINE: Bien, non.

FRÉDÉRIC: Où ________________?
SANDRINE: Il est avec sa soeur Catherine.
FRÉDÉRIC: Où?
SANDRINE: Au McDonald.
FRÉDÉRIC: Ah bon! Merci Sandrine. Salut!

CATHERINE: Tiens, Frédéric, ça va?
FRÉDÉRIC: Oui, ça va . . . ton frère n'est pas avec toi?

CATHERINE: Non, il est ________________.
FRÉDÉRIC: Ah bon! Salut!

CATHERINE: ________________!

FRÉDÉRIC: Bonjour, madame.
LA MÈRE: Bonjour, Frédéric.

FRÉDÉRIC: ________________ parler à Jean-Claude?

LA MÈRE: ________________. Il est en haut *(upstairs)*.

FRÉDÉRIC: Jean-Claude? ________________?

JEAN-CLAUDE: Eh, ben, oui. ________________ là.

CASSETTE WORKSHEET Leçon 14 (cont.)

| Section 6 | Prononciation |

G. *La voyelle /a/*

Écoutez: ch**a**t

The letter "**a**" alone always represents the sound /a/ as in the English word
ah. It never has the sound of "*a*" as in English words like *class, date,* or *cinema.*

Répétez: ch**a**t ç**a** v**a** **à** l**a** l**à**-b**a**s **a**vec **a**mi voil**à**
cl**a**sse c**a**fé s**a**l**a**de d**a**me d**a**te M**a**d**a**me C**a**n**a**d**a**
Anne est **a**u C**a**n**a**d**a** **a**vec M**a**d**a**me L**a**v**a**l.

À votre tour!

Section 7. Allô!

Allez à la page 104.

Section 8. Créa-dialogue

Allez à la page 104.

UNITÉ 4

Nom _______________________________________

Classe _________________________________ Date _____________

CASSETTE WORKSHEET Leçon 15 Une boum

| Section 1 | Une boum |

A. *Compréhension orale*

Jean-Marc has been invited to a party. He is trying to decide whether to invite Béatrice or Valérie. First he talks to Béatrice.

JEAN-MARC:	Dis, Béatrice, tu aimes danser?
BÉATRICE:	Bien sûr, j'aime danser!
JEAN-MARC:	Est-ce que tu danses bien?
BÉATRICE:	Oui, je danse très, très bien.
JEAN-MARC:	Et ta cousine Valérie? Est-ce qu'elle danse bien?
BÉATRICE:	Non, elle ne danse pas très bien.
JEAN-MARC:	Alors, c'est Valérie que j'invite à la boum.
BÉATRICE:	Mais pourquoi elle? Pourquoi pas moi?
JEAN-MARC:	Écoute, Béatrice, je ne sais pas danser! Alors, je préfère inviter une fille qui ne danse pas très bien. C'est normal, non?

B. *Écoutez et répétez.*

| Section 2 | J'étudie |

C. *Compréhension orale*

		A			B
▶	✓	J'étudie.			Je n'étudie pas.
1		J'étudie.			Je n'étudie pas.
2		Je travaille.			Je ne travaille pas.
3		Je travaille.			Je ne travaille pas.
4		Je regarde la télé.			Je ne regarde pas la télé.
5		Je joue au Monopoly.			Je joue au Nintendo.
6		Elle joue très mal.			Elle joue très bien.
7		Je mange.			Je ne mange pas.
8		Je mange un sandwich.			Je mange une omelette.
9		Je mange une crêpe.			Je mange une pizza.
10		J'écoute la radio.			J'écoute mon walkman.
11		Je téléphone.			Je ne téléphone pas.
12		Je téléphone à un copain.			Je téléphone à une copine.

UNITÉ 4

CASSETTE WORKSHEET   Leçon 15

Section 3   Tu téléphones?

D. *Compréhension orale*

1. Tu téléphones?

a. _____ oui   b. _____ non

2. Tu regardes la télé?

a. _____ oui   b. _____ non

3. Est-ce que tu étudies?

a. _____ oui   b. _____ non

4. Tu dînes à la maison ce soir?

a. _____ oui   b. _____ non

Section 4   Est-ce qu'il travaille?

E. *Questions et réponses*

▶ — Est-ce qu'il travaille?
   — **Non, il ne travaille pas.**

CASSETTE WORKSHEET Leçon 15 (cont.)

| Section 5 | Jean-Paul à la boum |

F. *Compréhension orale*

First Jean-Paul goes up to Dominique.

JEAN-PAUL: _________________________ danser?

DOMINIQUE: Oui, j'aime _________________ .

JEAN-PAUL: Est-ce que tu danses _________________ ?

DOMINIQUE: Oui, je danse très, très bien. Et toi?

JEAN-PAUL: Euh non, _________________ .

Then Jean-Paul goes over to Nathalie.

JEAN-PAUL: Tu aimes danser?

NATHALIE: Oui, j'aime danser . . . mais _________________ très bien.

JEAN-PAUL: _________________ danser avec moi?

NATHALIE: Je te dis (*I'm telling you*), je ne danse pas très bien.

JEAN-PAUL: Moi non plus (*me neither*), je ne danse pas _________________ .

NATHALIE: Bon, _________________ .

CASSETTE WORKSHEET Leçon 15 (cont.)

| Section 6 | **Prononciation** |

G. *Les voyelles /i / et /u /*

Écoutez: /u/ **où**   /i/ **ici**

The vowel sounds **/i/** and **/u/** are easy to say. Remember to pronounce the French "**i**" as in **Mimi** and not as in the English *him*.

Répétez: /i/   ici Philippe il
                 Mimi Sylvie visite
                 Philippe visite Paris avec Sylvie.

         /u/   où nous vous
                 écoute joue toujours
                 Vous jouez au foot avec nous?

À votre tour!

Section 7. Allô!

    Allez à la page 116.

Section 8. Créa-dialogue

    Allez à la page 116.

UNITÉ 4

Nom ____

Classe _________________________ Date _____________

CASSETTE WORKSHEET Leçon 16 Une interview

| Section 1 | **Une interview** |

A. *Compréhension orale*

Nicolas is at a café with his new friend Fatou. He's interviewing her for an article in his school newspaper.

NICOLAS: Bonjour, Fatou. Ça va?

FATOU: Oui, ça va.

NICOLAS: Tu es sénégalaise, n'est-ce pas?

FATOU: Oui, je suis sénégalaise.

NICOLAS: Où est-ce que tu habites?

FATOU: Je suis de Dakar, mais maintenant j'habite à Paris avec ma famille.

NICOLAS: Est-ce que tu aimes Paris?

FATOU: J'adore Paris.

NICOLAS: Qu'est-ce que tu fais le weekend?

FATOU: Ça dépend. En général, je regarde la télé ou je sors avec mes copains. Dis, Nicolas! Est-ce que je peux te poser une question?

NICOLAS: Oui, bien sûr!

FATOU: Qu'est-ce que tu fais samedi?

NICOLAS: Euh . . . je ne sais pas.

FATOU: Est-ce que tu veux aller avec nous à un concert de musique africaine?

NICOLAS: Super! Où? Quand? Et à quelle heure?

B. *Écoutez et répétez.*

CASSETTE WORKSHEET Leçon 16 (cont.)

Section 2 Où est-ce qu'il va?

C. Compréhension orale

	A	B	C	D	E	F
	où?	quand?	à quelle heure?	comment?	à qui?	avec qui?
▶	✓					
1						
2						
3						
4						
5						
6						
7						
8						

Section 3 Qu'est-ce que tu fais?

D. Compréhension orale

a. _____

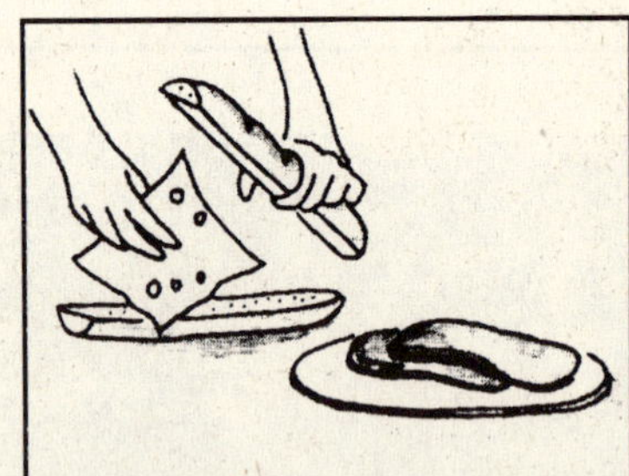

b. __1__

c. _____

d. _____

e. _____

f. _____

Nom _______________________________

CASSETTE WORKSHEET   Leçon 16   (cont.)

Section 4   Questions

E. *Questions et réponses*

▶ — Qu'est-ce qu'il mange?
   — **Il mange un sandwich.**

Section 5   Au Sénégal

F. *Écoutez et écrivez.*

— Bonjour, _______________________________ vous vous appelez?

— Je m'appelle Monsieur Li.

— _______________________ français?

— Oui, _______________________ français, et le ouolof aussi.

CASSETTE WORKSHEET   Leçon 16 (cont.)

| Section 6 | **Prononciation** |

G. *La voyelle /y/*
Écoutez: **su**per!

The vowel sound /y/, represented by the letter "**u,**" does not exist in
English. Here is a helpful trick for producing this new sound. First say the
French word **si.** Then round your lips as if to whistle and say **si** with
rounded lips: /**sy**/. Now say **si-per.** Then round your lips as you say the
first syllable: **super!**

Répétez: /y/   **su**per   **tu**   é**tu**die   bien **sûr**
          Lucie   **Lu**c
          Tu é**tu**dies avec **Lu**cie.

À votre tour!

Section 7. Allô!

   Allez à la page 126.

Section 8. Créa-dialogue

   Allez à la page 126.

WRITING ACTIVITIES Leçon 13 Le français pratique: Mes activités

A* 1. Qu'est-ce qu'ils aiment faire? *(What do they like to do?)*

The following people are saying what they like to do. Complete the bubbles, as in the model.

J'aime téléphoner.

2. Et toi?

Say whether or not you like to do the activities suggested by the pictures.

1. _______________________________
____
____

2. _______________________________
____
____

3. _______________________________
____
____

4. _______________________________
____
____

5. _______________________________
____
____

6. _______________________________
____
____

7. _______________________________
____
____

8. _______________________________
____
____

*NOTE: Beginning with this unit, activities are coded to
<u>sections</u> in your textbook (Ex: Leçon 13, Section A)
for your reference.

UNITÉ 4

WRITING ACTIVITIES Leçon 13 (cont.)

B/C 3. **Communication: En français!**

1. You are spending your vacation in a French summer camp.

   Ask your friend Patrick . . .
   - *if he likes to swim*

   ____

   - *if he likes to play basketball*

   ____

   - *if he wants to play volleyball with you*

   ____

2. Your friend Cécile is phoning to invite you to go to a restaurant. Unfortunately you have an English exam tomorrow.

   Tell Cécile . . .
   - *that you are sorry*

   ____

   - *that you cannot have dinner at the restaurant with her*

   ____

   - *that you have to study*

   ____

3. At the tennis court, you meet your friend Jean-Claude.
   - *Tell him that you would like to play tennis.*

   ____

   - *Ask him if he wants to play with you.*

   ____

WRITING ACTIVITIES   Leçon 14   Qui est là?

A 1. Mots croisés *(Crossword puzzle)*

Complete the crossword puzzle with the forms of **être.** Then write the corresponding subject pronoun in front of each form.

▶ nous ___________ S O M M E S

1. ___________ [ ] S

2. ___________ S [ ] S

3. ___________ [ ] [ ] [ ] S

4. ___________ S [ ] [ ] T

5. ___________ [ ] S [ ]

2. En vacances

The people in parentheses are on vacation. Say where they are, using the appropriate pronouns: **il, elle, ils,** or **elles.**

▶ (Cécile) _Elle est_ à Québec.

1. (Jean-Marc) ___________ à Tours.

2. (Catherine et Sophie) ___________ à Nice.

3. (Mademoiselle Simon) ___________ à Montréal.

4. (Jérôme et Philippe) ___________ en Italie.

5. (Isabelle, Thomas et Anne) ___________ au Mexique.

6. (Monsieur et Madame Dupin) ___________ au Japon.

3. Où sont-ils?

Complete the following sentences, saying where the people are.

Nous ___________________________ .

Vous ___________________________ .

M. Bernard ___________________________ .

Éric et Claire ___________________________ .

UNITÉ 4

WRITING ACTIVITIES Leçon 14 (cont.)

B/C **4. Non!**

Answer the following questions in the negative, using pronouns in your answers.

1. Est-ce que tu es français (française)?

____

2. Est-ce que ton copain est canadien?

____

3. Est-ce que ta copine est anglaise?

____

4. Est-ce que tu es au cinéma?

____

5. Est-ce que tes *(your)* parents sont en vacances?

____

5. **Communication: En français!**

1. The phone rings. It is your French friend Caroline who wants to talk to your brother.

   Tell Caroline that he is not home.

   ____

   Tell her that he is downtown with a friend.

   ____

2. You are phoning your friend Marc. His mother answers.

   Ask her if Marc is there.

   ____

   Ask her if you can please speak with Marc.

   ____

UNITÉ 4

WRITING ACTIVITIES Leçon 15 Une boum

A/B 1. Tourisme

The following people are traveling abroad. Complete the sentences
with the appropriate forms of **visiter.**

1. Nous _______________ Québec.

2. Tu _______________ Fort-de-France.

3. Jean et Thomas _______________ Paris.

4. Vous _______________ Genève.

5. Hélène _______________ San Francisco.

6. Je _______________ La Nouvelle Orléans.

7. Marc _______________ Tokyo.

8. Monsieur et Madame Dupont _______________ Mexico.

2. Qu'est-ce qu'ils font?

Describe what people are doing by completing the sentences with the
appropriate verbs. First write the infinitive in the box, and then fill in
the correct form in the sentence. Be logical.

| manger | **écouter** | *regarder* | **dîner** |
| jouer | organiser | **parler** | |

▶	dîner	Nous _____ dînons _____ au restaurant.
1.		Christine et Claire _______________ au tennis.
2.		Vous _______________ la télé.
3.		J'_______________ la radio.
4.		Tu _______________ français avec le professeur.
5.		Jérôme _______________ un sandwich.
6.		Nous _______________ une boum.

WRITING ACTIVITIES Leçon 15 (cont.)

3. Descriptions

Look carefully at the following scenes and describe what the different people are doing.

▶ Mélanie ___*nage*_________________ .   Monsieur Boulot _________________ .

Éric et Vincent _________________ .   Claire et Philippe _________________ .

Le professeur _________________ .   Diane _________________ .

Hélène et Marc _________________ .   Jean-Paul et Bernard _________________ .

WRITING ACTIVITIES Leçon 15 (cont.)

C **4. Et toi?**

Your French friend Caroline wants to know more about you. Answer her questions, affirmatively or negatively.

1. Tu parles anglais?

____

2. Tu parles souvent français?

____

3. Tu habites à New York?

____

4. Tu étudies l'espagnol?

____

5. Tu joues au foot?

____

6. Tu dînes souvent au restaurant?

____

5. Dimanche

For many people, Sunday is a day of rest. Say that the following people are not doing the activities in parentheses.

▶ (étudier)   Tu _______ *n'étudies pas* _______ .

1. (étudier)   Nous _____________________ .

2. (travailler)   Vous _____________________ .

3. (parler)   Mon copain _______________ français.

4. (téléphoner)   La secrétaire _____________ .

5. (jouer)   Paul et Thomas ___________ au foot .

6. (voyager)   Tu _______________________ .

WRITING ACTIVITIES Leçon 15 (cont.)

6. Communication

You have a new French pen pal named Isabelle. Write her a short letter introducing yourself.

Date your letter.

- *Tell Isabelle your name.*

- *Tell her in which city you live.*

- *Tell her at what school you study.*

- *Tell her whether or not you often speak French.*

- *Tell her what sports you play.*

- *Tell her two things you like to do.*

- *Tell her one thing you do not like to do.*

Sign your letter.

Chère Isabelle,

____

Amitiés,

Nom ____

Classe _______________________________ Date _____________

WRITING ACTIVITIES Leçon 16 Une interview

A 1. Dialogue

Complete the following dialogues with the appropriate interrogative expressions.

1. —_________________________ est-ce que tu habites?
   —J'habite à Dakar.

2. —_________________________ est-ce que tu dînes?
   —En général, je dîne à huit heures.

3. —_________________________ est-ce que tu chantes?
   —Je chante assez bien.

4. —_________________________ est-ce que tu étudies l'italien?
   —Parce que je veux visiter l'Italie.

5. —_________________________ est-ce que tu voyages?
   —Je voyage en juillet.

6. —_________________________ est-ce que ta mère travaille?
   —Elle travaille dans *(in)* un hôpital.

B 2. Répétitions

Philippe did not quite hear what Annie told him and he asks her to repeat what she said. Complete his questions.

ANNIE:		PHILIPPE:
▶ Je joue au tennis avec Vincent.	Avec	*qui est-ce que tu joues au tennis* ?
1. Je téléphone souvent à Olivier.	À	?
2. Je parle rarement à Valérie.	À	?
3. J'étudie avec Jean-Claude.	Avec	?
4. Je travaille pour M. Bertrand.	Pour	?
5. Je parle anglais avec Vanessa.	Avec	?
6. Je parle de Pierre.	De	?

UNITÉ 4

WRITING ACTIVITIES Leçon 16 (cont.)

A/B/C 3. Curiosité

You want to know more about what the following people are doing. Write your questions using subject pronouns and the expressions in parentheses.

▶ Jérôme dîne. (avec qui?)

Avec qui est-ce qu'il dîne?

1. Madame Martin travaille. (où?)

____

2. Nathalie téléphone. (à qui?)

____

3. Antoine organise une boum. (quand?)

____

4. Thomas et Patrick étudient beaucoup. (pourquoi?)

____

5. Hélène et Sylvie jouent au tennis. (à quelle heure?)

____

6. Béatrice étudie. (qu'est-ce que?)

____

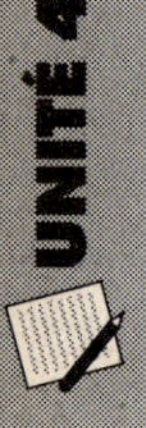

UNITÉ 4

D 4. Conversations

Complete the following mini-dialogues with the appropriate forms of **faire.**

1. —Qu'est-ce que tu _________ à deux heures?

   —Je _________ un match de tennis.

2. —Qu'est-ce que vous _________ maintenant?

   —Nous _________ une salade de fruits.

3. —Où est ta cousine?

   —Elle _________ un voyage au Sénégal.

4. —Où sont Paul et Marc?

   —Ils sont en ville. Ils _________ une promenade.

WRITING ACTIVITIES Leçon 16 (cont.)

5. Communication

1. You want to invite your friend Nathalie to your home for dinner.

   Ask her . . .

   • *at what time she has dinner* ____

   • *what she likes to eat* ____

2. You are interviewing Madame Ricard, a French businesswoman, for your school newspaper.
   (Do not forget to address her as **vous!**)

   Ask her . . .

   • *where she lives* ____

   • *where she works* ____

   • *when she travels* ____

3. You meet your friend Marc in the street.

   Ask him . . .

   • *what he is doing now* ____

   • *what he is doing tomorrow* ____

UNITÉ 4

READING AND CULTURE ACTIVITIES Unité 4

A. En France et en Louisiane

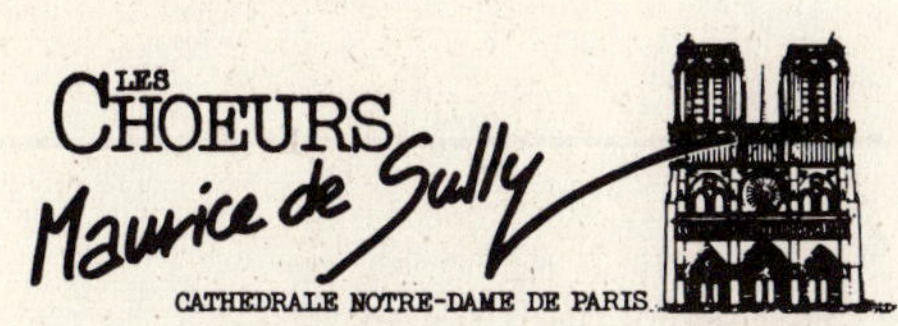

1. You would pay attention to this ad
if you were interested in . . .
- ☐ singing
- ☐ traveling
- ☐ going to a concert
- ☐ visiting a church

2. If you were traveling in Louisiana, you
might see this sign in certain shops.
What does it mean?
- ☐ We are French.
- ☐ French is spoken here.
- ☐ We sell French products.
- ☐ We like French people.

3. Here is another sign you might see in
Louisiana. What does it mean?
- ☐ We do not speak French.
- ☐ We are proud to speak French.
- ☐ We sell French products.
- ☐ We love people who speak French.

READING AND CULTURE ACTIVITIES Unité 4 (cont.)

B. La Maison des Jeunes et de la Culture

Sandrine Moreau has dropped by Les Marquisats to get more
information about their activities. She was asked to fill out the
following form.

Je souhaite recevoir régulièrement des informations sur les activités culturelles
de la Maison des Jeunes et de la Culture "Les Marquisats" d'Annecy.

Je suis plus particulièrement intéressé par :

☐ CINÉMA   ☑ DANSES SPÉCIALES   ☐ CONFÉRENCES

☑ STAGES DANSE   ☐ JAZZ   ☐ ROCK   ☐ CHANSON

NOM *MOREAU, Sandrine*

INSTITUTION / PROFESSION *Étudiante*

ADRESSE *136, rue Descartes*

Annecy

TÉL. ______________ (facultatif).

LES **M**ARQUISATS
M. J. C.   52, RUE DES MARQUISATS
74000 ANNECY   TEL. 04.50.45.08.80

---

1. Sandrine is especially interested in . . .
  ☐ movies
  ☐ music
  ☐ dance
  ☐ lectures

2. Who is Sandrine?
  ☐ A student.
  ☐ A homemaker.
  ☐ A guitarist.
  ☐ A retired person.

READING AND CULTURE ACTIVITIES Unité 4 (cont.)

C. Conversation

Carefully read the following phone conversation between Carole and
her friend Julien.

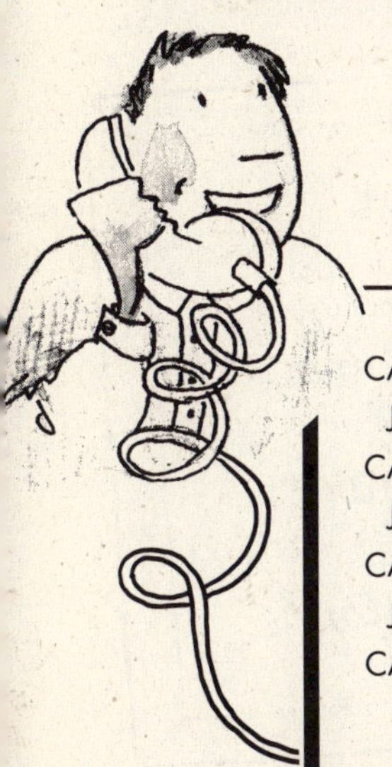

CAROLE: Allô, Julien?
JULIEN: Ah, c'est toi, Carole. Mais où es-tu?
CAROLE: Je suis à Tours.
JULIEN: À Tours? Mais pourquoi es-tu là-bas?
CAROLE: Je fais un voyage avec ma cousine.
JULIEN: Ah bon! Qu'est-ce que vous faites?
CAROLE: Oh là là, nous faisons beaucoup de choses. Nous visitons
les châteaux. Nous dînons dans les restaurants.
Nous . . .
JULIEN: Quand est-ce que vous rentrez à Paris?
CAROLE: Le quinze août.
JULIEN: Alors, bonnes vacances et bon retour!

- Where is Carole when she calls Julien? _______________________________________

  Where is Julien? ____

- With whom is Carole traveling? ____

- What have the two of them been doing?

  ____

  ____

- When is Carole returning home? ____

READING AND CULTURE ACTIVITIES Unité 4 (cont.)

D. Invitations

1. You recently received two invitations. (Note: **venir** means *to come*.)

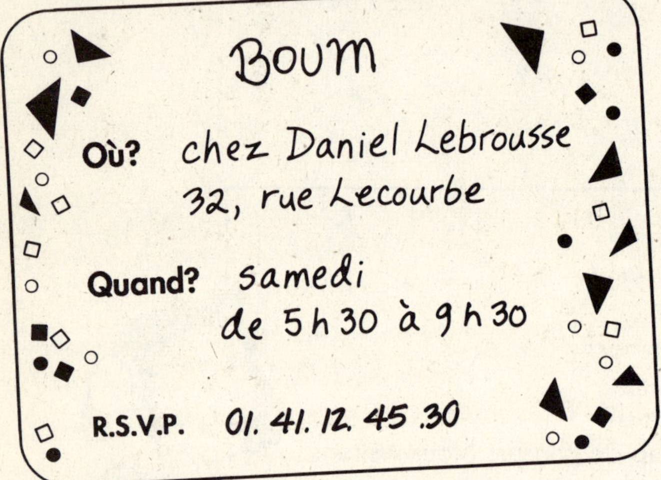

- What is Daniel's invitation for? _______________________________

  What day and what time? _______________________________

- What is Christophe's invitation for? _______________________________

  What day and what time? _______________________________

- Which invitation are you going to accept, and why?

  ____

  ____

2. Write a note to the person whose invitation you have to turn down.
- Express your regret.
- Explain that you have other plans.
- Sign your note.

Cher _____________,

____

____

____

____

____

COMMUNICATIVE EXPRESSIONS AND THEMATIC VOCABULARY
Unité 4   Qu'est-ce qu'on fait?

▶ CULTURAL CONTEXT: **Daily activities at home, at school, on weekends**

COMMUNICATIVE EXPRESSIONS

Talking about what you like and don't like to do
Qu'est-ce que tu aimes faire?
Est-ce que tu aimes . . . ?
    J'aime . . .   Je n'aime pas . . .
    Je préfère . . .

Talking about what you want and do not want to do
Qu'est-ce que tu veux faire?
    Je veux . . .   Je ne veux pas . . .
    Je voudrais . . .

Inviting a friend
Est-ce que tu veux . . . ?   . . . avec moi/toi
Est-ce que tu peux . . . ?

Accepting and turning down an invitation
Oui, bien sûr, . . .   Je regrette mais je ne peux pas.
Oui, merci, . . .   Je dois . . .
Oui, d'accord, . . .
    je veux bien.
    je veux bien . . .

Asking and answering yes/no questions
Est-ce que [tu étudies]?   oui   non
[Tu étudies], n'est-ce pas?   mais oui   mais non
                bien sûr
                peut-être . . .

Asking for specific information
où?   Où est-ce que tu habites?
quand?   Quand est-ce que tu regardes la télé?
à quelle heure?   À quelle heure est-ce que tu dînes?
comment?   Comment est-ce que tu joues au volley?
pourquoi?   Pourquoi est-ce que tu étudies le français?
    parce que . . .   Parce que je veux visiter Paris.

qu'est-ce que . . . ?   Qu'est-ce que tu fais?

qui?   Qui travaille?
                Qui est-ce que tu invites?
à qui?   À qui est-ce que tu téléphones?
de qui?   De qui est-ce que tu parles?
avec qui?   Avec qui est-ce que tu joues au tennis?
pour qui?   Pour qui est-ce que tu travailles?

COMMUNICATIVE EXPRESSIONS AND THEMATIC VOCABULARY

VOCABULARY

Things people do

aimer	manger	faire
chanter	nager	faire un match
danser	organiser une boum	faire une promenade
dîner au restaurant	parler anglais	faire un voyage
écouter la radio	parler espagnol	faire attention
étudier	parler français	
habiter à [Québec]	regarder la télé	être
inviter	téléphoner	être d'accord
jouer au basket	travailler	
jouer au foot	visiter [Paris]	
jouer au tennis	voyager	
jouer au volley		

Places where one can be

où	à [Paris]	en France
ici	à la maison	en classe
là	au café	en vacances
là-bas	au cinéma	en ville
	au restaurant	

How well? how much? how often? when?

bien	beaucoup	rarement	maintenant
très bien	un peu	souvent	
mal		toujours	

Other words and expressions

à	avec	super!
de	mais	dommage!
et	pour	
ou		ah bon?

UNITÉ 5
Le monde personnel et familier

LISTENING ACTIVITIES
Leçons 17–20

WRITING ACTIVITIES
Leçons 17–20

READING AND CULTURE ACTIVITIES
Unité 5

POUR COMMUNIQUER

Communicative Expressions and Thematic Vocabulary

Nom _______________________________

Classe _________________________ Date ___________

CASSETTE WORKSHEET Leçon 17 Le français pratique:
Les personnes et les objets

| Section 1 | **La description des personnes** |

A. *Écoutez et répétez.*

Allez à la page 139.

| Section 2 | **J'ai un walkman** |

B. *Compréhension orale*

a. ____

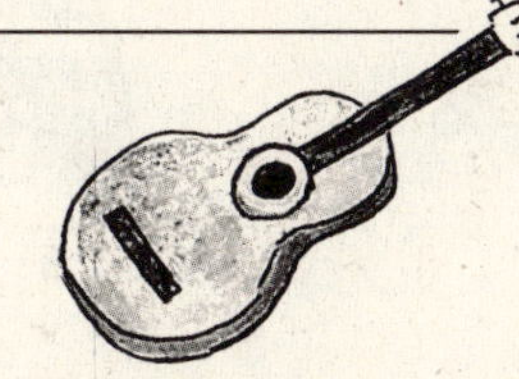

b. ____

c. ____

d. ____

e. __1__

f. ____

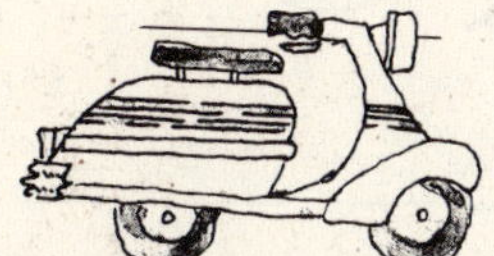

g. ____

h. ____

i. ____

j. ____

k. ____

l. ____

UNITÉ 5

CASSETTE WORKSHEET Leçon 17 (cont.)

| Section 3 | Qu'est-ce que c'est? |

C. *Questions et réponses*

▶ — Qu'est-ce que c'est?
  — **C'est un appareil-photo.** ▶ 

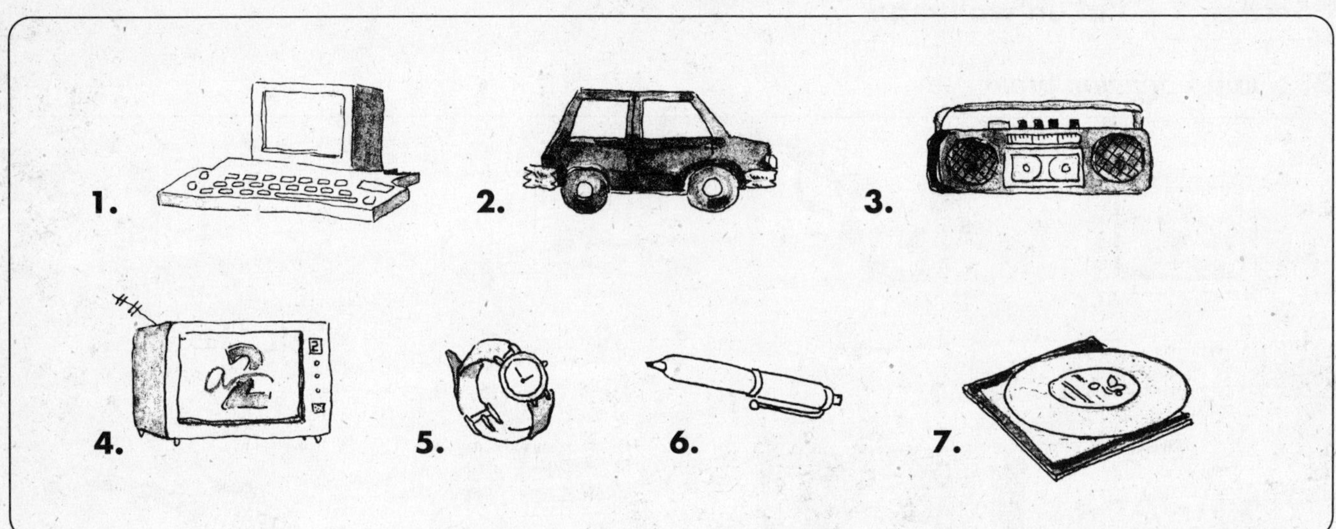

1. 2. 3.

4. 5. 6. 7.

| Section 4 | Dialogue: Tu as un walkman? |

D. *Compréhension orale*

1. Nathalie a un walkman.   vrai   faux

2. Le walkman est dans son sac.   vrai   faux

3. Le sac est sur la table.   vrai   faux

4. Le sac est dans sa chambre.   vrai   faux

5. Le sac est sous son bureau.   vrai   faux

6. Le sac est derrière la porte. vrai   faux

UNITÉ 5

Nom _______________________________

CASSETTE WORKSHEET Leçon 17 (cont.)

| Section 5 | Où est-il? |

E. *Questions et réponses*

▶ — Est-ce que l'appareil-photo est sur la table ou sous la table?
   — Il est sur la table.

CASSETTE WORKSHEET Leçon 17 (cont.)

| Section 6 | **Monologue: La chambre de Catherine** |

F. *Compréhension orale*

a. ☐ un bureau
b. ☐ une chaise
c. ☐ une table
d. ☐ un lit
e. ☐ des disques
f. ☐ des affiches
g. ☐ des livres
h. ☐ un livre de français
i. ☐ un livre d'anglais
j. ☐ un sac de classe

k. ☐ des crayons
l. ☐ un stylo
m. ☐ une calculatrice
n. ☐ un cahier
o. ☐ un ordinateur
p. ☐ une raquette
q. ☐ une radiocassette
r. ☐ des compact-discs
s. ☐ un appareil-photo

À votre tour!

Section 7. Créa-dialogue

Allez à la page 147.

Section 8. Conversation dirigée

Allez à la page 147.

UNITÉ 5

DISCOVERING FRENCH – *BLEU*

CASSETTE WORKSHEET Leçon 18 Vive la différence!

Section 1 Vive la différence!

A. *Compréhension orale*

Listen to Caroline, a French girl from Montpellier, describe herself and her friend Jean-Pierre.

Je m'appelle Caroline.	Il s'appelle Jean-Pierre.
J'habite à Montpellier.	Il habite à Strasbourg.
J'ai des frères.	Il n'a pas de frère, mais il a des soeurs.
J'ai un chien.	Il n'a pas de chien, mais il a deux horribles chats.
J'ai un scooter.	Il a une moto.
J'aime le cinéma.	Il préfère le théâtre.
J'aime les films de science-fiction.	Il préfère les westerns.
J'aime les sports.	Il préfère la musique.
J'étudie l'anglais.	Il étudie l'espagnol.

B. *Écoutez et répétez.*

Section 2 Tu as un vélo?

C. *Compréhension orale*

▶ un vélo (oui) non

1. a. un vélo oui non
   b. une mobylette oui non

2. une voiture oui non

3. une voiture oui non

4. une montre oui non

UNITÉ 5

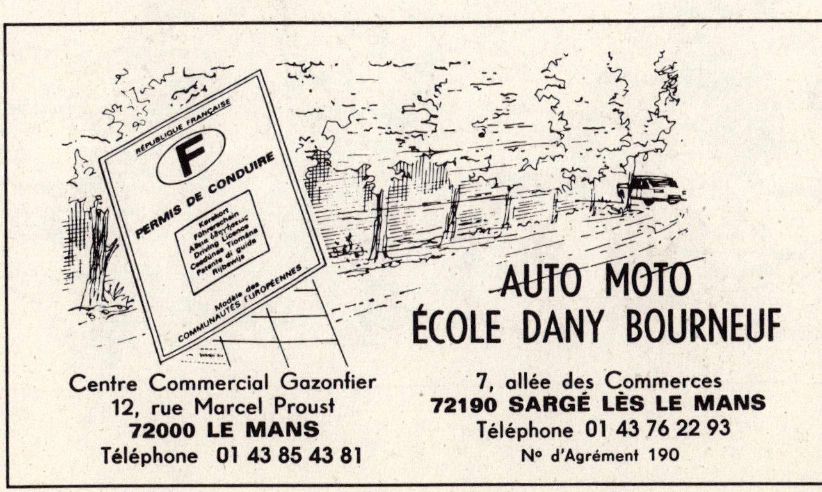

CASSETTE WORKSHEET   Leçon 18   (cont.)

| Section 3 | Qu'est-ce que tu as? |

D. *Compréhension orale*

1. a. un stylo   oui   non
    b. des crayons   oui   non
    c. un cahier   oui   non
    d. une calculatrice oui   non
    e. des livres   oui   non
    f. un sandwich   oui   non

2. a. un crayon   oui   non
    b. un stylo   oui   non

3. a. un walkman   oui   non
    b. des cassettes   oui   non

4. a. une calculatrice oui   non
    b. un ordinateur   oui   non

5.   une raquette   oui   non

UNITÉ 5

CASSETTE WORKSHEET   Leçon 18   (cont.)

Section 4 | **Est-ce que tu as un vélo?**

E. *Questions et réponses*

▶ —Est-ce que tu as un vélo?
—**Oui, j'ai un vélo.**
(Non, je n'ai pas de vélo.) ▶

1.

2.

3.

4.

5.

6.

7.

Section 5 | **Dialogue: J'organise une boum**

F. *Compréhension orale*

1. une chaîne stéréo   oui   non
2. une radiocassette   oui   non
3. des cassettes   oui   non
4. des compact-discs   oui   non
5. un vélo   oui   non
6. une mobylette   oui   non

UNITÉ 5

CASSETTE WORKSHEET   Leçon 18 (cont.)

| **Section 6** | **Prononciation** |

G. *Les articles* le *et* les

Écoutez: <u>**le**</u> sac   <u>**les**</u> sacs

Be sure to distinguish between the pronunciation of **le** and **les.** In spoken French, that is often the only way to tell the difference between a singular and a plural noun.

Répétez: /lə/   le   le sac   le vélo   le disque   le copain   le voisin

/le/   le**s**   le**s** sac**s**   le**s** vélo**s**   le**s** disque**s**   le**s** copain**s**   le**s** voisin**s**

Section 7. Allô!

   Allez à la page 158.

Section 8. Créa-dialogue

   Allez à la page 158.

Nom ____

Classe ____ Date _____________

CASSETTE WORKSHEET Leçon 19 Le copain de Mireille

Section 1 | **Le copain de Mireille**

A. *Compréhension orale*

Nicolas and Jean-Claude are having lunch at the school cafeteria. Nicolas is looking at the students seated at the other end of the table.

NICOLAS: Regarde la fille là-bas.
JEAN-CLAUDE: La fille blonde?
NICOLAS: Oui! Qui est-ce?
JEAN-CLAUDE: C'est Mireille Labé.
NICOLAS: Elle est mignonne!
JEAN-CLAUDE: Oui, elle est aussi amusante, intelligente et très sympathique.
NICOLAS: Est-ce qu'elle a un copain?
JEAN-CLAUDE: Oui, elle a un copain.
NICOLAS: Il est sympathique?
JEAN-CLAUDE: Très sympathique!
NICOLAS: Et intelligent?
JEAN-CLAUDE: Aussi!
NICOLAS: Dommage! . . . Qui est-ce?
JEAN-CLAUDE: C'est moi!
NICOLAS: Oh . . . Excuse-moi et félicitations!

B. *Écoutez et répétez.*

Section 2 | **Je suis américain**

C. *Compréhension orale*

▶  a. américain   b. américaine

1. 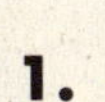 a. anglais   b. anglaise

2.  a. canadien   b. canadienne

3.  a. chinois   b. chinoise

4.  a. japonais   b. japonaise

5. 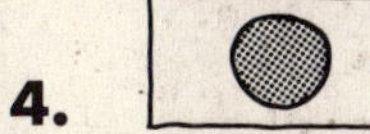 a. italien   b. italienne

6. 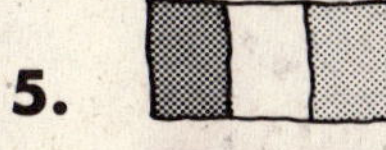 a. mexicain   b. mexicaine

CASSETTE WORKSHEET Leçon 19 (cont.)

| Section 3 | La description |

D. *Écoutez et répétez.*

Allez à la page 163.

| Section 4 | Qui est-ce? |

E. *Compréhension orale*

▶ (a.) mignon   b. mignonne

  (c.) sympathique   d. sympathiques

1. a. américains   b. américaines

     c. sympathique   d. sympathiques

2. a. espagnol   b. espagnole

     c. mexicaine   d. mexicaines

     e. sportif   f. sportive

     g. intelligente   h. intelligentes

3. a. anglais   b. anglaise

     c. américain   d. américaines

     e. intéressant   f. intéressante

     g. strict   h. strictes

UNITÉ 5

CASSETTE WORKSHEET Leçon 19 (cont.)

| Section 5 | **Comment sont-ils?** |

F. *Questions et réponses*

▶ — Est-ce qu'elle est grande ou petite?
— **Elle est grande.**

UNITÉ 5

CASSETTE WORKSHEET   Leçon 19 (cont.)

| Section 6 | Prononciation |

G. *Les consonnes finales*

Écoutez: **blon~~d~~**   **blon<u>d</u>e**

As you know, when the last letter of a word is a consonant, that consonant is often silent. But when a word ends in "e," the consonant before it is pronounced. As you practice the following adjectives, be sure to distinguish between the masculine and the feminine forms.

	MASCULINE ADJECTIVE (no final consonant sound)		FEMININE ADJECTIVE (final consonant sound)
Répétez:	**blon~~d~~**	/d/	**blon<u>d</u>e**
	gran~~d~~		**gran<u>d</u>e**
	peti~~t~~	/t/	**peti<u>t</u>e**
	amusan~~t~~		**amusan<u>t</u>e**
	françai~~s~~	/z/	**françai<u>s</u>e**
	anglai~~s~~		**anglai<u>s</u>e**
	américain	/n/	**américai<u>n</u>e**
	canadien		**canadie<u>nn</u>e**

À votre tour!

Section 7. Allô!

Allez à la page 168.

Section 8. Créa-dialogue

Allez à la page 168.

CASSETTE WORKSHEET Leçon 20 La voiture de Roger

| Section 1 | Dialogue: La voiture de Roger |

A. *Compréhension orale*

Dans la rue, il y a une voiture rouge.
C'est une petite voiture. C'est une voiture de sport.

Dans la rue, il y a aussi un café.
Au café, il y a un jeune homme.
Il s'appelle Roger.
C'est le propriétaire de la voiture rouge.

Une jeune fille entre dans le café.
Elle s'appelle Véronique.
C'est l'amie de Roger.
Véronique parle à Roger.

ROGER: Tiens, bonjour Véronique! Ça va?
VÉRONIQUE: Oui, ça va. Dis, tu as une nouvelle voiture, n'est-ce pas?
ROGER: Oui, j'ai une nouvelle voiture.
VÉRONIQUE: Est-ce qu'elle est grande ou petite?
ROGER: Oh, c'est une petite voiture.
VÉRONIQUE: De quelle couleur est-elle?
ROGER: C'est une voiture rouge.
VÉRONIQUE: Est-ce que c'est une voiture italienne?
ROGER: Oui, c'est une voiture italienne. Mais, dis donc, Véronique, tu es vraiment très curieuse!
VÉRONIQUE: Et toi, tu n'es pas assez curieux!
ROGER: Ah bon? Pourquoi?
VÉRONIQUE: Pourquoi? . . . Regarde la contractuelle là-bas!
ROGER: Ah, zut alors!

B. *Écoutez et répétez.*

| Section 2 | Les couleurs |

C. *Écoutez et répétez.*

 Allez à la page 172.

| Section 3 | De quelle couleur? |

D. *Compréhension orale*

a. _____ rouge   **b.** _____ jaune   **c.** _____ vert(e)   **d.** _____ blanc (blanche)

e. _____ gris(e)   **f.** _____ noir(e)   **g.** _____ marron   **h.** _____ orange

UNITÉ 5

CASSETTE WORKSHEET   Leçon 20   (cont.)

| Section 4 | Qu'est-ce que tu préfères? |

E. *Questions et réponses*

▶ —Est-ce que tu préfères la voiture rouge ou la voiture grise?
—**Je préfère la voiture rouge.**
(Je préfère la voiture grise.)

▶ 

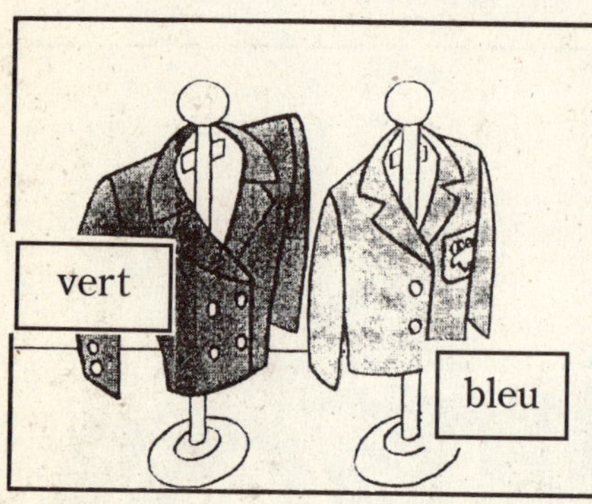

1.

2.

3.

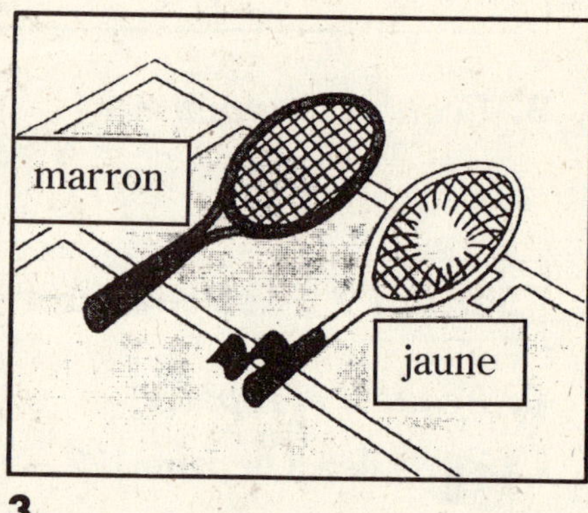

4.

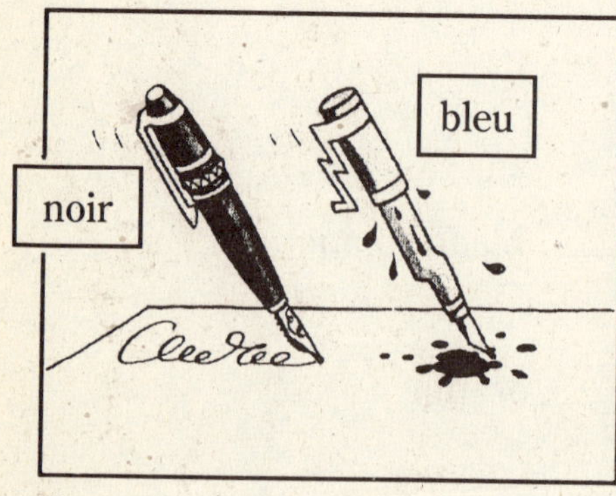

5.

6.

UNITÉ 5

CASSETTE WORKSHEET Leçon 20 (cont.)

| Section 5 | **Descriptions** |

F. *Écoutez et répétez.*

Allez à la page 173.

| Section 6 | **Dialogue: C'est ta voiture?** |

G. *Compréhension orale*

1. C'est la voiture de Jean-Claude.   vrai   faux
2. C'est une Citroën.   vrai   faux
3. Elle marche très bien.   vrai   faux
4. Elle n'est pas rapide.   vrai   faux
5. Elle fait du 160 à l'heure *(160 kilometers per hour)*.   vrai   faux
6. Jean-Claude a son permis *(driver's license)*.   vrai   faux

| Section 7 | **Prononciation** |

H. *Les lettres «ch»*

Écoutez: **chien**

The letters "**ch**" are usually pronounced like the English *"sh."*

Répétez: **chien   chat   chose   marche
chouette   chocolat   affiche
Michèle a un chat et deux chiens.**

UNITÉ 5

CASSETTE WORKSHEET   Leçon 20   (cont.)

À votre tour!

Section 8. Allô!

   Allez à la page 178.

Section 9. Créa-dialogue

   Allez à la page 178.

UNITÉ 5

Nom ____

Classe _________________________________   Date _____________

WRITING ACTIVITIES Leçon 17   Le français pratique: Les personnes et les objets

A 1. Auto-portrait

Write a short paragraph describing yourself. Give the following information:

- your name
- your age
- two physical traits

2. Mes acteurs favoris

Describe your favorite actor and actress by completing the following chart. Use complete sentences.

	MON ACTEUR FAVORI	**MON ACTRICE FAVORITE**
- name	Il _______________	Elle _______________
- age (approx.)		
- physical traits (affirmative or negative)		

3. Communication

1. Your French friend Sophie has a new neighbor and you want to know more about him.

   Ask Sophie . . .

   - *his name*
   - *how old he is*
   - *if he is tall or short*
   - *if he is good-looking*

2. Your friend Christophe has just told you that one of his cousins—a girl—is going to visit him next week.

   Ask Christophe . . .

   - *her name*
   - *if she is blond or brunette*
   - *if she is pretty*

UNITÉ 5

WRITING ACTIVITIES Leçon 17 (cont.)

B/C **4. L'intrus** *(The intruder)*
The following sentences can be completed logically by three of the items A, B, C, and D. One item does not fit. It is the intruder. Cross it out.

	A	B	C	D
1. Dans le garage, il y a…	une voiture	un vélo	une chambre	un scooter
2. Dans le sac, il y a…	un disque	une porte	un walkman	un appareil-photo
3. Sur le bureau, il y a…	un ordinateur	une calculatrice	un téléphone	une chaise
4. Sur le mur *(wall)*, il y a…	une affiche	une montre	une photo	un poster
5. Sur la table, il y a…	un crayon	une radio	un stylo	une mobylette
6. Dans la chambre, il y a…	une moto	une table	deux chaises	une chaîne stéréo
7. Sous le lit, il y a…	un scooter	un livre	des compacts	un chat

5. Quatre listes
Complete each list with three items.

What I carry in my school bag: 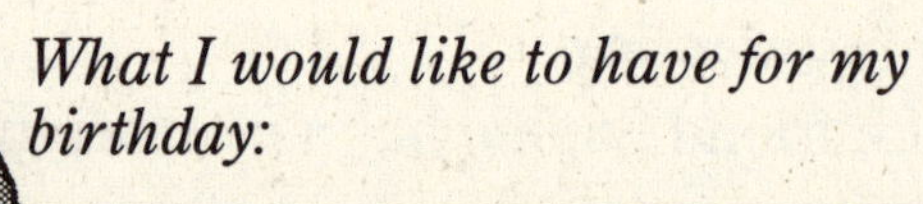

- _______________________
- _______________________
- _______________________

What I would like to have for my birthday: 

- _______________________
- _______________________
- _______________________

What I would take on a trip to Paris: 

- _______________________
- _______________________
- _______________________

What I would want to have if I were lost on a desert island: 

- _______________________
- _______________________
- _______________________

WRITING ACTIVITIES Leçon 17 (cont.)

6. Leurs possessions *(Their belongings)*

Look at the illustrations and describe four things that each of the
following people own. Be sure to use **un** or **une,** as appropriate.

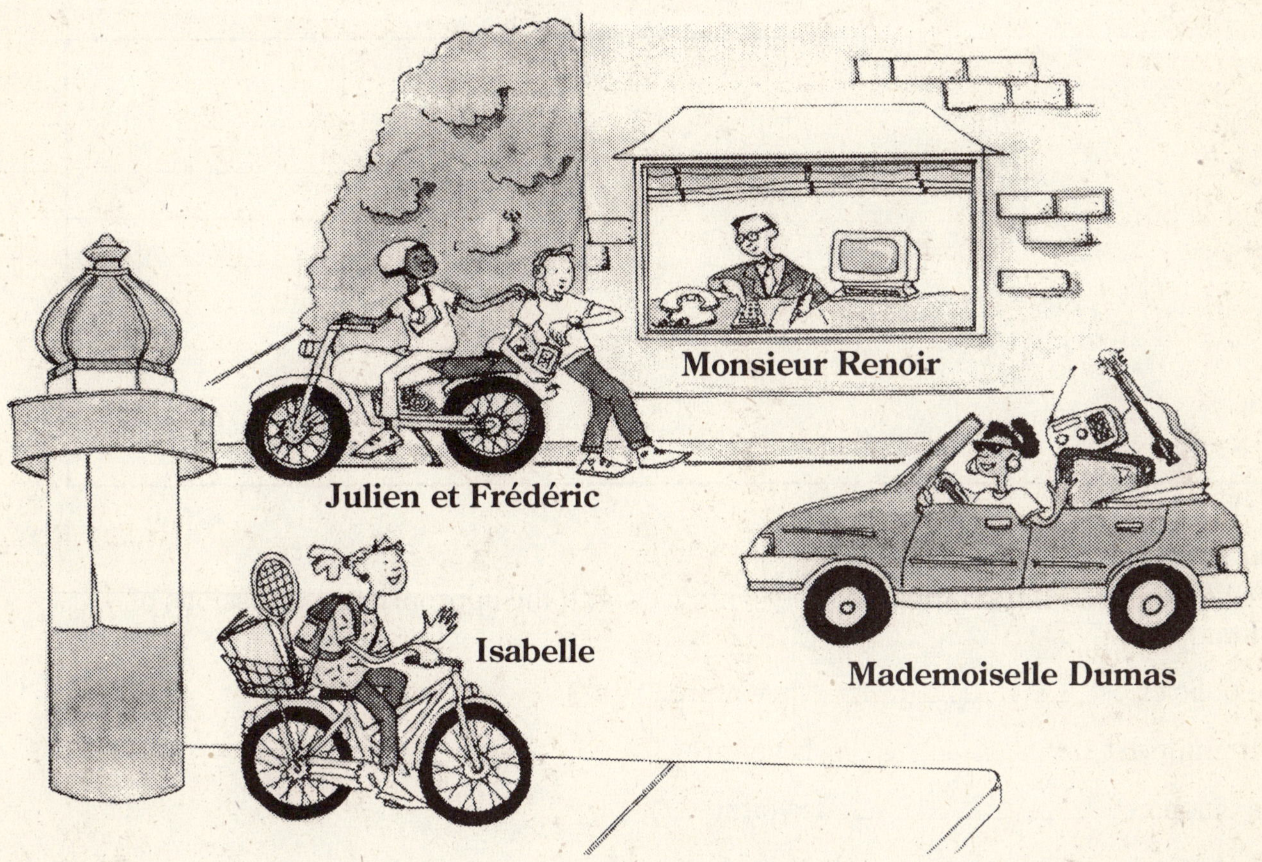

1. Isabelle a *(has)* un vélo, ____ .

2. Mademoiselle Dumas a ____ .

3. Julien et Frédéric ont *(have)* ____

____ .

4. Monsieur Renoir a ____

____ .

UNITÉ 5

WRITING ACTIVITIES Leçon 17 (cont.)

D 7. Ma chambre

Make a floor plan of your room, indicating the position of the door,
the window(s), and the various pieces of furniture. Label everything
in French.

8. Où sont-ils?

Describe the cartoon by completing the sentences with the appropriate expressions of
location.

1. Le policier est _________________ la voiture.

2. L'homme est _________________ la voiture.

3. Le chien est _________________ la voiture.

4. Le chat est _________________ la voiture.

5. Le vélo est _________________ la voiture.

WRITING ACTIVITIES Leçon 18 Vive la différence!

A 1. Au café

A group of friends is at a café. Read what everyone is ordering. Then say if they are hungry or thirsty, using the appropriate forms of **avoir faim** or **avoir soif.**

▶ Hélène commande *(orders)* un jus de tomate. _Elle a soif._

1. Nous commandons une pizza. _______________________

2. Je commande une limonade. _______________________

3. Tu commandes un steak-frites. _______________________

4. Patrick commande un sandwich. _______________________

5. Vous commandez un jus de raisin. _______________________

6. Pauline et Sophie commandent un soda. _______________________

B 2. Au choix *(Your choice)*

Complete the sentences with one of the suggested nouns. Be sure to use **un** or **une,** as appropriate.

▶ Éric mange _une pizza (un sandwich)_ . (sandwich? pizza?)

1. Nathalie commande _______________________ . (glace? soda?)

2. Sophie écoute _______________________ . (cassette? disque?)

3. J'écris *(write)* avec _______________________ . (crayon? stylo?)

4. Pour mon anniversaire, je voudrais _______________________ . (vélo? radiocassette?)

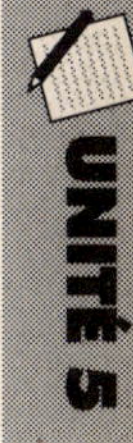

UNITÉ 5

Nom ____

WRITING ACTIVITIES Leçon 18 (cont.)

C 3. Quel article?

Complete the following sentences with the suggested articles, as appropriate.

(un, une, des)

1. Dans le garage, il y a _______ voiture et _______ bicyclettes.

2. Dans ma chambre, il y a _______ chaises et _______ lit.

3. Thomas a _______ cassettes et _______ magnétophone.

4. Isabelle est _______ copine. Paul et Marc sont _______ copains.

(le, la, l', les)

5. _______ élèves et _______ professeur sont dans la classe.

6. _______ ordinateur est sur _______ bureau.

7. _______ livres sont sur _______ table.

8. Où sont _______ cassettes et _______ disques?

D 4. Pourquoi pas?

Sometimes we do not do certain things because we do not have what we need. Read about what the following people do not do. Then explain why by saying that they do not have one of the things in the box.

une télé	**une voiture**	*une radio*
une raquette	une montre	un livre

▶ Monsieur Dumont ne voyage pas.   Il n'a pas de voiture. ____________

1. Claire ne regarde pas le match de foot. ____________________________

2. Paul ne joue pas au tennis. ____________________________

3. Henri n'écoute pas le concert. ____________________________

4. Sophie n'étudie pas. ____________________________

5. Jean n'est pas ponctuel *(punctual)*. ____________________________

UNITÉ 5

WRITING ACTIVITIES Leçon 18 (cont.)

E 5. Qu'est-ce que tu préfères?

Indicate your preferences by choosing one of the items in parentheses.
(Note: * = a feminine singular noun; ** = a plural noun)

▶ (soda ou limonade*?) *Je préfère la limonade (le soda).*

1. (théâtre ou cinéma?) __________________________________

2. (musique* ou sports**?) __________________________________

3. (gymnastique* ou volley?) __________________________________

4. (français ou maths**?) __________________________________

5. (pizza* ou spaghetti**?) __________________________________

6. (carottes** ou salade*?) __________________________________

F 6. Quel jour?

Say on which days of the week you do the following things.

▶ J'ai une classe de maths *le mardi et le jeudi* _____________ .

1. J'ai une classe de français __________________________________ .

2. J'ai une classe de musique __________________________________ .

3. Je dîne au restaurant __________________________________ .

4. Je fais les courses (*go shopping*) __________________________________ .

	LUNDI	MARDI	MERCREDI	JEUDI	VENDREDI	SAMEDI
8h30 à 9h30	Histoire	Allemand		Sciences économiques		Français
9h30 à 10h30	Anglais	Français	Anglais	Sciences physiques	Allemand	Français
10h30 à 11h30	Sport	Français	Sciences économiques	(13h30) Maths	Latin	Latin
11h30 à 12h30	Français	Latin	Maths	(13h30)	Sciences physiques	Histoire ou Civilisation
13h00 à 14h00		Maths		Allemand		
14h00 à 15h00	Sciences physiques	Maths		Histoire		
15h00 à 16h00	Géographie	Anglais				
16h00 à 17h00	Civilisation					

UNITÉ 5

WRITING ACTIVITIES Leçon 18 (cont.)

7. Communication: En français!

1. You want to organize a party but you need help with the music.
   You phone your friend Mélanie.

   - *Tell her that you do not have a stereo.* ______________________________

   - *Ask her if she has a tape recorder.* ______________________________

   - *Ask her if she has cassettes.* ______________________________

2. You have invited Stéphanie to your house.

   - *Ask her if she is thirsty.* ______________________________

   - *Ask her if she likes orange juice.* ______________________________

   - *Ask her if she wants to watch TV.* ______________________________

Nom ____

Classe _____________________________ Date _____________

WRITING ACTIVITIES Leçon 19 Le copain de Mireille

A 1. Frères et soeurs

The following brothers and sisters are like each other. Describe the sisters, according to the model.

▶ Alain est blond.   Monique *est blonde* _______________________ .

1. Marc est petit.   Yvonne _______________________________ .

2. Philippe est grand.   Françoise ____________________________ .

3. Jean-Claude est timide. Stéphanie ____________________________ .

4. Pierre est intelligent. Alice _______________________________ .

5. Paul est sympathique.   Juliette _____________________________ .

6. Jérôme est beau.   Hélène ______________________________ .

7. Julien est mignon.   Céline ______________________________ .

8. Patrick est sportif.   Catherine ___________________________ .

2. Cousin, cousine

Describe two cousins of yours, one male, one female. Write four sentences for each person. (Your sentences may be affirmative or negative.)

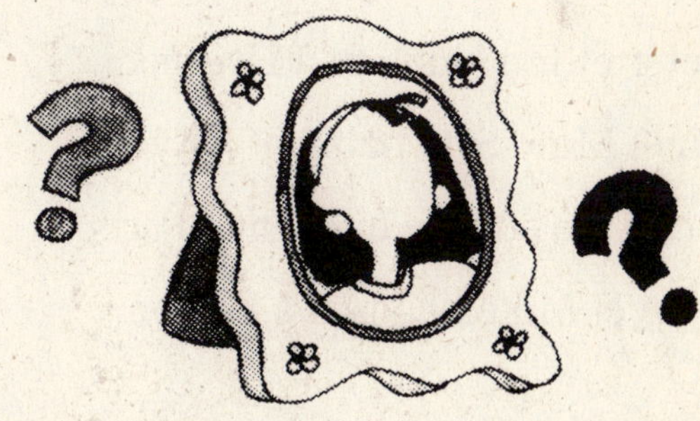

▶ Il n'est pas très grand.   Elle est assez mignonne.

Mon cousin s'appelle _____________ .   Ma cousine s'appelle _____________ .

1. ______________________________   1. ______________________________

2. ______________________________   2. ______________________________

3. ______________________________   3. ______________________________

4. ______________________________   4. ______________________________

UNITÉ 5

WRITING ACTIVITIES Leçon 19 (cont.)

A/B **3. Descriptions**

Complete the following descriptions with **le, la,** or **les** and the appropriate forms of the adjectives in parentheses.

▶ _Les_ livres sont ___intéressants___ .   (intéressant)

1. ___ cassette est _________________ .   (intéressant)

2. ___ livres sont _________________ .   (amusant)

3. ___ table est _________________ .   (grand)

4. ___ chambre est _________________ .   (petit)

5. ___ chiens sont _________________ .   (gentil)

4. Quelle nationalité?

Read where the people live and give their nationalities. (Be sure to give the appropriate form of the adjective.)

▶ Madame Li habite à Hong Kong.   Elle ___est chinoise___ .

1. Anne et Marie habitent à Québec.   Elles _________________ .

2. Madame Suárez habite à Mexico.   Elle _________________ .

3. Mon cousin habite à Zurich.   Il _________________ .

4. Silvia et Maria habitent à Rome.   Elles _________________ .

5. Peter et Jim habitent à Liverpool.   Ils _________________ .

6. M. et Mme Sato habitent à Kyoto.   Ils _________________ .

7. Delphine et Julie habitent à Paris.   Elles _________________ .

8. John et Mike habitent à Boston.   Ils _________________ .

UNITÉ 5

WRITING ACTIVITIES Leçon 19 (cont.)

C 5. Les voisins

Sandrine is talking about her neighbors. Write what she says using
the words in parentheses. Follow the model.

▶ (fille / amusant)　　　Catherine _____*est une fille amusante*_____.

1. (garçon / timide)　　　Charles _______________________________.

2. (amie / gentil)　　　Véronique _______________________________.

3. (homme / sympathique)　M. Dupont _______________________________.

4. (femme / intelligent)　　Mme Bérard _______________________________.

A/B/C 6. Commérages *(Gossip)*

Jean-Paul likes to talk about other people. Write what he says, using
the suggested words.

▶ Philippe / avoir / amie / japonais

Philippe a une amie japonaise.

1. Frédéric / inviter / fille / anglais

____

2. Jacques et Olivier / dîner avec / amies / canadien

____

3. Bernard / téléphoner à / copine / mexicain

____

4. Le professeur / avoir / élèves / bête

____

5. Jean-Pierre / avoir / livres / intéressant

____

UNITÉ 5

WRITING ACTIVITIES Leçon 19 (cont.)

7. Communication

Write a short letter in French in which you describe yourself and two of your best friends.

UNITÉ 5

WRITING ACTIVITIES Leçon 20 La voiture de Roger

A 1. Drapeaux de pays francophones *(Flags of French-speaking countries)*
Color the flags according to the instructions.

B L E U	B L A N C	R O U G E

France

N O I R	J A U N E	R O U G E

Belgique

O R A N G E	B L A N C	V E R T

Côte d'Ivoire

2. De quelle couleur?
Describe the colors of the following items. (Use your imagination, if necessary.)

▶ Mon jean est _________ bleu _________.

1. Mon tee-shirt est _______________________ .

2. Mon crayon est _______________________ .

3. Ma chambre est _______________________ .

4. Ma bicyclette est _______________________ .

5. Mon chien est _______________________ .

6. La voiture de ma famille est _______________ .

UNITÉ 5

WRITING ACTIVITIES Leçon 20 (cont.)

B 3. Descriptions

Complete the following descriptions by writing in the appropriate form of one of the adjectives from the box.

bon	**mauvais**	grand	**beau**	petit

▶ San Francisco est une ___belle (grande)___ ville *(city)*.

1. New York est une _______________ ville.

2. J'habite dans une _______________ ville.

3. Ma famille a une _______________ voiture.

4. J'ai une _______________ chambre.

5. Les Red Sox sont une _______________ équipe *(team)*.

6. Les Cowboys sont une _______________ équipe.

7. Le président est un _______________ président.

4. Le Rallye cycliste

A group of friends is bicycling together. Each one has a different bicycle. Describe the bicycles using the suggested adjectives.

▶ Éric a ___un vélo anglais___. (anglais)

▶ Isabelle a ___un grand vélo___. (grand)

1. Philippe a _______________. (italien)

2. Thomas a _______________. (rouge)

3. Claire a _______________. (petit)

4. Hélène a _______________. (vert)

5. Marc a _______________. (joli)

6. Laure a _______________. (japonais)

UNITÉ 5

WRITING ACTIVITIES Leçon 20 (cont.)

C **5. Panne sèche** *(Out of ink)*

Nathalie had planned to stress certain words by writing them in red ink. She realized—too late—that her red pen had dried up. Complete her assignment by filling in the missing words: **c'est, il est,** or **elle est.**

1. Voici Jean-Pierre.

   _______________ un copain.

   _______________ canadien.

   _______________ un garçon sympathique.

2. Voici Madame Leblanc.

   _______________ une voisine.

   _______________ une personne intéressante.

   _______________ très intelligente.

3. Regarde la voiture là-bas.

   _______________ une voiture française.

   _______________ une Renault.

   _______________ petite et rapide.

4. J'ai un scooter.

   _______________ rouge.

   _______________ italien.

   _______________ un bon scooter.

UNITÉ 5

WRITING ACTIVITIES Leçon 20 (cont.)

D 6. Opinions personnelles

Here is a list of activities. Choose three activities you like and one
activity you do not like. Explain why, using adjectives from the box.

ACTIVITÉS:

- danser
- chanter
- nager
- jouer au foot
- jouer au basket
- voyager

- visiter les musées
- organiser des boums
- inviter des copains
- étudier
- parler français
- travailler à la maison

chouette	**pénible**
super	**facile**
extra	**difficile**
drôle	

▶ J'aime organiser les boums. C'est chouette! ________________

▶ Je n'aime pas visiter les musées. C'est pénible. ____________

1. ____

2. ____

3. ____

4. ____

7. 👥 Communication: La voiture familiale *(The family car)*

Write a short description of your family car—or the car of someone
you know. You may want to answer the following questions—in
French, of course!

- *What make is it?* ________________________________

- *Is it an American car?* ___________________________

  (if not, what is it?) _____________________________

- *What color is it?* _______________________________

- *Is it large or small?* ____________________________

- *Is it a good car?* _______________________________

UNITÉ 5

Nom ____

Classe _________________________________ Date ______________

READING AND CULTURE ACTIVITIES Unité 5

A. En France

1. You would go to this place if you had a problem with your . . .
- ☐ bicycle
- ☐ watch
- ☐ car
- ☐ computer

2. This is an ad for . . .
- ☐ a book
- ☐ a cassette
- ☐ a concert
- ☐ a TV program

3. According to this ad, which of the following items could you buy at this store?
- ☐ A tape recorder.
- ☐ A typewriter.
- ☐ A computer.
- ☐ A movie camera.

READING AND CULTURE ACTIVITIES Unité 5 (cont.)

4. The following ad was placed by Parmelan, which is the name of . . .
- ☐ a hotel
- ☐ a travel agency
- ☐ a phone company
- ☐ a TV store

5. You would buy this magazine if you were interested in . . .
- ☐ music
- ☐ photography
- ☐ history
- ☐ computers

6. According to the ad, this would be the place to go if you wanted to buy . . .
- ☐ used records
- ☐ secondhand typewriters
- ☐ stereo equipment
- ☐ old clothes

UNITÉ 5

READING AND CULTURE ACTIVITIES Unité 5 (cont.)

B. Articles à vendre

You are in France and have gone to the local supermarket. There,
on the board, you see the following announcements for items for sale.

> **OCCASION EXCEPTIONNELLE**
> **vends**
> **Appareil-photo OLYMPUS AM 100**
> **avec Flash intégré**
> **Prix: 50€**
> **Téléphoner à Sophie Lebihan**
> **01.49.22.61.32**

- What is Sophie selling? ____

  What price is she asking? ____

- How can you reach her? ____

> **À VENDRE**
> **Vélo tout terrain**
> **10 vitesses**
> **Excellente condition**
> **Prix: à débattre**
> **Téléphoner à Didier Muller**
> **entre 16 heures et 19 heures**
> **03. 88. 22. 61. 32**

- What is Didier selling? ____

  What price is he asking? ____

- When can you reach him? ____

READING AND CULTURE ACTIVITIES Unité 5 (cont.)

C. Le club des Correspondants

You have been looking at a French youth magazine and noticed the following requests for pen pals.

Le club des Correspondants

Garçon français,
16 ans, brun, yeux bleus, sympathique mais un peu timide, voudrait correspondre avec Américaine ou Anglaise parlant le français. Aime le sport, le ciné et la moto. Joindre photo. Réponse assurée.
   Olivier Lambesq
   25, place Gambetta
   24100 Bergerac

Jeune Américain,
16 ans, voudrait correspondre avec jeunes Français du même âge parlant l'anglais. Aime le ciné, la musique classique et la moto. Joindre photo. Réponse assurée.
   Patrick Smith
   1329 Cole Street
   San Francisco, CA 94117

Jeune Française,
15 ans, sportive (tennis, basket, ski) désire correspondre avec étudiants américains ou anglais du même âge pour échanger posters et cassettes de rock et de rap.
Écrire à:
   Dominique Loiseau
   32, rue du Dragon
   75006 Paris

Je m'appelle Julie,
et j'ai douze ans. Je voudrais correspondre avec un garçon canadien de 13 à 15 ans, parlant anglais, pour échanger cassettes. J'aime le jazz, le rock et le rap.
   Julie Cartier
   25, rue Colbert
   63000 Clermont-Ferrand.

J'aime la danse,
le cinéma et la musique. J'ai 16 ans et je suis française. Je voudrais correspondre avec fille ou garçon de mon âge, de préférence porto-ricain ou mexicain, pour échanger cassettes de musique latine ou de guitare espagnole.
   Carole Gaune
   45, boulevard de la Mer
   76200 Dieppe, France

Mots croisés

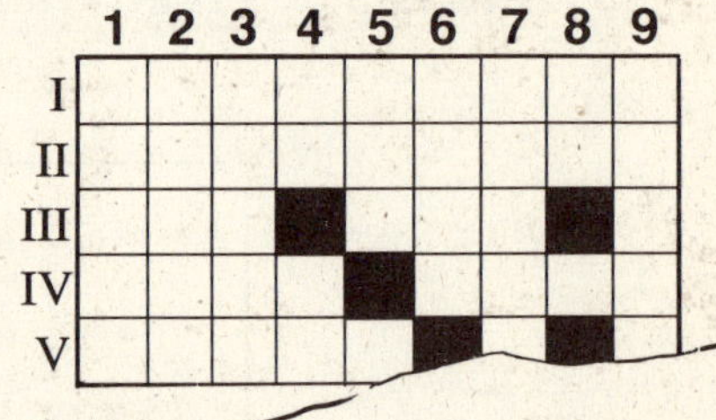

- Which of the young people like music?

   ____

   Which one does not mention music? ________________________

- Which ones want to trade things? ________________________

   What do they want to trade? ________________________

- Which ones mention sports? ________________________

- Would you like to correspond with any of these young people?

   Why or why not? ________________________

UNITÉ 5

COMMUNICATIVE EXPRESSIONS AND THEMATIC VOCABULARY

Unité 5 Le monde personnel et familier

▶ CULTURAL CONTEXT: **People and their possessions**

COMMUNICATIVE EXPRESSIONS

Asking what things people have
> Est-ce que tu as . . . ?
>> Oui, j'ai . . .
> Non, je n'ai pas (de) . . .

Asking what there is
> Qu'est-ce qu'il y a?
> Est-ce qu'il y a . . . ?
>> Il y a . . .
>> Il n'y a pas (de) . . .

Asking where something is
> Où est . . . ?
>> Il/Elle est | dans . . .
>> sur . . .
>> sous . . .
>> devant . . .
>> derrière . . .

Asking if something works
> Est-ce qu'il/elle marche?

Saying that you know or do not know
> Je sais.
> Je ne sais pas.

Giving an opinion on an activity
> C'est . . .

chouette	bien
difficile	mal
drôle	
extra	
facile	
faux	
pénible	
super	
vrai	

VOCABULARY

People

des gens	une personne
un camarade	une camarade
un élève	une élève
un étudiant	une étudiante
un homme	une femme
un professeur	
un voisin	une voisine

Objects and things

un objet — une chose

un appareil-photo	un sac	une affiche	une montre
un compact	un scooter	une auto	une moto
un crayon	un stylo	une bicyclette	une radio
un disque	un téléphone	une calculatrice	une radiocassette
un livre	un vélo	une cassette	une raquette
un magnétophone	un walkman	une chaîne stéréo	une télé
un ordinateur		une guitare	une voiture
		une mobylette	

UNITÉ 5

COMMUNICATIVE EXPRESSIONS AND THEMATIC VOCABULARY

VOCABULARY (continued)

In a room

une chambre	un bureau	une chaise
une fenêtre	un lit	une table
une porte		

Description of people

- *physical features*

beau, belle	grand	joli
blond	jeune	petit
brun		

- *personality traits*

amusant	intéressant	sportif, sportive
bête	méchant	sympathique
gentil, gentille	mignon, mignonne	timide
intelligent		

- *nationalities*

américain	espagnol	japonais
anglais	français	mexicain
canadien, canadienne	italien, italienne	suisse
chinois		

Colors

De quelle couleur est . . . ?

blanc, blanche	noir
bleu	orange
gris	rose
jaune	rouge
marron	vert

Other descriptions

bon, bonne	mauvais

Verbs

avoir	marcher
avoir faim	
avoir soif	

Other words and expressions

assez	si *(yes)*	le lundi	alors
très		le weekend	dis!
			dis donc!